Bullcroft, Carcroft & Askern

Early Development

Dave Fordham

Fedj-el-Adoum Publishing

Published by Fedj-el-Adoum Publishing
3 Adelaide Road, Norton, Doncaster, South Yorkshire, DN6 9EW

Copyright © Dave Fordham 2009

ISBN 978-0-9562864-2-0
First Edition 2009

All rights reserved. No part of this publication may be reproduced, stored in a retrieval system, or transmitted, in any form or by any means, electronic, mechanical, photocopying, recording, or otherwise without written permission of the author.

Cover Illustration:

Bullcroft Colliery in 1912. This postcard is one of a series that were produced by an anonymous photographer to depict the newly developed colliery. The workers have successfully replaced the old wooden framed headgears with the two steel lattice headgears pictured. Note the scale of the massive headgears in comparison with the height of the workers. The colliery is now ready to start full production.

Bullcroft Colliery Carcroft & Skellow

Early Development

Bullcroft Colliery in 1914

Acknowledgements

The author would like to thank the following for their assistance in compiling this work:

John Fordham, Joan Ulley & Paul Fox for suggesting improvements to the manuscript; Stan Longley; BarnSCAN - *The Barnsdale Local History Group*; the staff of Doncaster Archives; Helen Wallder and Carol Hill from Doncaster Local Studies Library for allowing access to contemporary newspaper records from *The Doncaster Gazette* and *The Doncaster Chronicle;* the staff of The National Coal Mining Museum for England Library and The University of Birmingham Library for viewing their holdings of *The Colliery Guardian;* The Historical Model Railway Society; the Library of The London School of Economics & Political Science for allowing the reproduction of the photograph of the Markham family; and the many picture postcard publishers whose work has been used to illustrate this publication, in particular Edgar Leonard Scrivens and James Simonton & Sons. Unless otherwise attributed, all illustrations featured in this publication are from the author's collection.

Bullcroft Main Colliery

Prior to the development of Bullcroft Colliery, the village of Carcroft was a small rural settlement comprising stone built cottages, a couple of farms, a chapel and the old Moon Inn. There was no church as villagers walked across Owston Park to the parish church in the estate village of Owston where the Davis-Cooke family owned Owston Hall. A mile to the west could be found a similar agricultural settlement called Skellow centred on the old Butter Cross and the bridge over a small stream known as the River Skell.

At the beginning of the 20th Century, Carcroft was a rural village comprising stone built agricultural labourer's cottages, a chapel and a couple of farms. This is High Street in 1908 recorded as a postcard by Edgar Scrivens. All of the cottages depicted have since been demolished to make way for the D.F.S. / Northern Upholstery furniture showrooms).

However, this peaceful rural scene was to be shattered in the first years of the 20th Century when there was a scramble to secure coal leases from the local landed gentry, as various colliery companies sought to raise the capital to sink pits and construct housing estates for the workforce.

The first colliery concern with an interest in the Carcroft area was the Don Coal & Iron Co. Ltd. who, in 1903, secured the lease of coal beneath 12,000 acres of land belonging to the Anne family of Burghwallis Hall and the Davies-Cooke family of Owston Hall. In addition to the Carcroft area, The Don Coal & Iron Co. managed to secure coal leases over a large tract of land between Askern and Pontefract where they had plans to develop a series of pits, their first project being Askern Colliery. However, the Don Coal & Iron Co. was having trouble raising the money to develop their ambitious plans and in 1908 they sold their lease in the Carcroft area to Arthur Markham, the Liberal M.P. for Mansfield.

At the time Arthur Markham was scouting the Doncaster area in an attempt to secure coal leases in order to extract the famous Barnsley Coal Seam. He was a director of the Hickleton Main Colliery Co. Ltd. who had recently opened Brodsworth Main Colliery (where he was the Chairman) in a joint venture with Staveley Coal & Iron Co. Ltd. of Chesterfield. The Chairman of the Staveley Company was Charlie Markham, Arthur's older brother.

On April 17th 1908 the Bullcroft Main Colliery Co. Ltd. was formed with a capital of £150,000 to acquire form Arthur Markham the coal lease that he had secured from the Don Coal & Iron Co Ltd. The first signatories were:

Arthur Markham, 48 Portland Place, London (Chairman)
Mrs Lucy Markham, 48 Portland Place, London (Arthur Markham's wife)
Charlie Markham, Harland Hall, Chesterfield (Managing Director)
Miss Violet Markham, Tapton House, Chesterfield
Henry Westlake, Brimington Hall, Chesterfield
William Bird, 58 Cadogan Place, London
William Humble, Bolsover

The whole of the £150,000 capital was provided independently by the Markham family and thus Bullcroft Main Colliery was a private venture controlled by Arthur Markham (who had the largest shareholding), his wife Lucy, his brother Charlie Markham and their sister Violet Markham. In fact for a couple of years the colliery was known as Markham's Pit before the name Bullcroft came into common usage. The Markham family were vastly influential in the development of the colliery industry in this country and Arthur and Charlie's father, Charles Markham had given his name to the large Markham Colliery near Bolsover in Derbyshire which was owned by the Staveley Coal & Iron Co. Ltd. Simultaneously with Bullcroft, Arthur Markham was involved with the development of Markham Colliery in South Wales for the Tredegar Coal & Iron Co. Ltd. of which he was a director, and this colliery would also take the family name. Returning to South Yorkshire, Arthur Markham would give his name to another colliery at Armthorpe near Doncaster, thus there would come to be three Markham Collieries, one in Derbyshire, another in South Wales and finally Markham Main in South Yorkshire.

Of the other directors of the Bullcroft Main Colliery Co. Ltd., Henry Westlake and William Bird were directors of The Staveley Coal & Iron Co. Ltd. where Charlie Markham was the Chairman. William Humble was appointed pit manager and he moved from Bolsover to take up residence at Skellow Grange where he would oversee the sinking of the new colliery. A site at Carcroft was chosen for the colliery adjacent to the Great Northern and Great Central Railway's line from Doncaster to Leeds and over the next two months equipment for sinking the colliery was transported to the new site by rail.

Above: The Markham family at Stuffynwood Hall near Mansfield, 1904. Standing in the centre is Rosa Markham (the daughter of the Crystal Palace architect Joseph Paxton), with her children Arthur (holding baby Joy), Charles and Violet. Seated on the far right is Arthur's wife Lucy Markham. In 1907 Arthur & Lucy Markham moved to fashionable Portland Place in London whilst retaining another home at Newstead Abbey near Mansfield. (Copyright London School of Economics Library File Ref: LSE/Markham/21/8).

*The coal seams beneath the Carcroft area were leased from the estates of the Anne family of Burghwallis Hall and the Davies-Cooke family of Owston Hall. The Anne family left Burghwallis Hall in 1941 and the house is now used as a convent by the Sisters of Charity of Our Lady of Good and Perpetual Succour. The Davies-Cooke family finally sold Owston Hall in the 1980s although the building had been converted into flats and is now a hotel and restaurant. (**Above:** Postcard by Edgar Scrivens; **Below:** Postcard by unknown photographer, Stan Longley Collection).*

In June 1908 a small ceremony to cut the first sod for the sinking of Bullcroft Colliery took place. It was announced that two shafts would be sunk and they were expected to reach the Barnsley Coal Seam at a depth of 600 yards. When fully completed, the pit would produce up to 5,000 tons of coal per day and 1,000,000 tons of coal per year. This output was intended to be produced by a workforce of 3,000 miners. The shafts would be sunk by a team lead by William Humble and the sinkers who had just completed Brodsworth Colliery would move over to the new site. Two headgears constructed from massive wooden beams would be built above the Bullcroft shafts to aid the sinking process.

Early days at Bullcroft Main Colliery, as depicted on a postcard by an unknown photographer c1908. The Union Jack appears to be flying from the top of the headgear, usually indicative of reaching coal, but in this case it probably signifies the cutting of the first sod beneath the wooden headgear above No. 1 shaft. The wooden headgear for No. 2 shaft has yet to be constructed; the smaller headgear is probably raising water from a borehole for use on the site.

Bullcroft Colliery was not the first pit that the Markham family had developed and owned outright. In the 1890s they had opened a small colliery at Oxcroft near Bolsover in Derbyshire although this was on a much smaller scale than Bullcroft as it only employed around 1,000 men. At Bullcroft, it was not deemed necessary to sink a borehole to prove the coal measures as the nearby

Brodsworth and Bentley Collieries had already struck the Barnsley Coal Seam. In retrospect, this proved to be a bad decision not to drill test boreholes as these would have displayed the problems with incursions of water that would be encountered in sinking the shafts, an inconvenience that had already been experienced a couple of years earlier at nearby Bentley Colliery.

This postcard by Edgar Scrivens from around 1909 depicts the sinking operations at Bullcroft Colliery. The shafts were sunk using the wooden headgears pictured which were intended to draw the coal once full production commenced. However, the Mines Act (1911) banned the use of wood for all future headgear structures and although the ones at Bullcroft could remain as they had been built before 1911, it was nevertheless decided to replace them with modern steel lattice headgears. (Stan Longley Collection).

The optimism of the colliery owners would soon be dampened in more ways than one, when in January 1909 the shafts at a depth of 33 yards started to fill up with water which had to be pumped out a rate of 1,000 gallons per minute. This was successfully blocked by lining the shafts with tubbing and sinking continued to a depth of 55 yards when the following month they encountered what Arthur Markham described as 'a subterranean river' when the shafts intercepted a cave system in the limestone. This influx of water drowned out the pumps at the bottom of the shafts. In April 1909 more powerful electric pumps were installed which could handle 6,000 gallons per minute but even these proved unsuccessful and in July 1909 the shafts had filled with water up to the surface and the sinking was suspended by the colliery company whilst Arthur Markham contacted experts in this engineering field.

The problem with the water inundation was largely due to the underlying geology. At Brodsworth the shafts were located on solid bedrock and shaft sinking was relatively straight forward. However, at Bullcroft the bedrock was buried beneath 30 yards of waterlogged glacial sediments which had filled the pre ice-age valley of the Hampole Beck. Beneath the unconsolidated sediments was the limestone bedrock. However, the upper beds of the limestone were rotten and fractured and full of cavities through which water flowed. Arthur Markham had no option but to call in experts from Belgium, Holland and Germany who had the experience of sinking through waterlogged sands, muds and fissured strata.

Towards the end of 1909, an offshoot of a German engineering company called The Shaft Freezing Company arrived on the site to take over the operations. They imported a team of German workers who during 1910 commenced the drilling of 28 boreholes positioned in a circular pattern around the shafts. They intended to pass a coolant through the boreholes which would have the effect of forming an ice wall surrounding the shafts which would then enable shaft sinking to continue through the frozen strata and down through the fractured limestone and onto solid bedrock.

During August 1910 the freezing process had been completed and the German team returned to the continent and the original pit sinkers recommenced work. However, the freezing work had not been totally successful as water began seeping into the shafts again and Arthur Markham recalled the German experts. This time in addition to freezing the water they drilled additional boreholes and injected quick drying cement into the porous sediments and this work was completed by November 1910 when sinking was restarted. The shafts had reached a depth of 100 yards by January 1911 when they were lined with iron tubbing to stem any leaks. Following this work sinking the shafts continued at a rapid and successful pace without any further incident. The additional expenditure incurred in sinking the shafts had caused the company to increase its capital to £300,000.

The problems with the sinking process and how they were overcome is thoroughly described in the book *Friendship's Harvest* by Violet Markham, Arthur Markham's sister. In her account Violet also mentions the site of water flowing out of the top of the shafts and following the freezing process she recalls standing in the shaft when beneath her feet was a solid column of ice. In retrospect, the drilling of preliminary boreholes would have saved Arthur Markham a lot of trouble and expense in the sinking of the Bullcroft shafts.

On Saturday 16th December 1911, Bullcroft Colliery reached the Barnsley coal seam at a depth of 662 yards. Arthur Markham stated that the thickness of coal, around 8 feet, was rather disappointing but he felt that the quality was right. He announced that the wooden headgears would be replaced with steel ones following the recent Mines Act (1911) and the surface buildings would be ready by June 1912 by which time the pit would be able to deal with a large output. The Company had purchased a large plot of land adjacent to Owston Park where a new village would be developed.

Bullcroft Colliery c1911 as shown on a postcard by Edgar Scrivens. The two brick built winding engine houses are connected by the power house and adjacent chimney and are in position ready to wind coal once the Barnsley seam is reached. Unlike other Doncaster area collieries, the chimney at Bullcroft was unusually short and would later be replaced with a much taller structure. Smoke is being emitted from a small chimney which served the temporary winding engines which were used to sink the shafts.

At the end of 1912, the Bullcroft Colliery Co. Ltd. was restructured by the Markham family and renamed Bullcroft Main Collieries Ltd. and the Markham's other colliery at Oxcroft was placed under Bullcroft control. The registered office of the new company was at Bullcroft Main Colliery, Carcroft, and the capital of the new venture was increased from £300,000 to £600,000. This was because Arthur Markham had recently secured a coal lease from Mr James Milnthorpe of The Hatfield Chase Corporation and it was his intention that this would be worked by Bullcroft Main Collieries from a new colliery at Barnby Dun near Doncaster, hence the increase in capital to provide funds for this proposal. This new pit was initially referred to as 'The Bullcroft Extension'.

Some of the first miners at Bullcroft Colliery in 1912. Four men are standing in the kibble, a large metal bucket which was used to remove the spoil from sinking the shafts. The kibble would be replaced with an iron cage which would be used to raise coal filled tubs from the base of the shaft. (Postcard, photographer unknown, Stan Longley Collection).

During 1913, Bullcroft Colliery was rapidly stepping up to maximum production and 1,000 miners were now employed. The shafts had been continued to a depth of 682 yards where they met the Dunsil Coal Seam. To protect the surface buildings from the effects of subsidence a shaft pillar, 750 yards in radius had been left in the Barnsley Coal Seam through which headings and roadways had been made to extract the coal beyond this by the longwall method of mining.

Two postcards by Edgar Scrivens depicting Bullcroft Colliery with steel headgear c1914. **Above:** No 1 & 2 shafts showing the covered gantries along which coal was transported to the screening plant and washery off camera to the left. **Below:** The frontage to Skellow Road with the main office block. The original short chimney is about to be made redundant by the newly constructed larger chimney to the left. This was necessary because the winding engines were now working flat out as in 1914 Bullcroft produced an annual output of 1,000,000 tons for the first time.

On the surface a pair of headgears of steel lattice construction had been built by the engineering company Markham & Co. of Chesterfield in Derbyshire who specialised in constructing colliery buildings and steam winding engines. Not surprisingly, this company was also connected to the Markham family being entirely owned by Charlie Markham. The two steam driven winding engines, supplied by Markham & Co. were housed in a pair of identical engine houses linked by a powerhouse with an adjacent chimney. Coal would be carried from the shaft tops to a German built *'Luhrig'* coal washery and screening plant before being dispatched into railway wagons as the Great Central Railway had now completed the sidings. Waste material was conveyed away by an aerial ropeway and tipped on to the meadows of Skellow Ings.

Many of the first miners at Bullcroft Colliery came from the Markham family's other colliery at Oxcroft in Derbyshire which had nearly exhausted its coal seams. Other men came to work at the pit from the surrounding farms and villages as well as from all over the country and by 1914 the colliery was producing 24,000 tons of coal per week and in that year the 2,500 miners produced over 1,000,000 tons of coal for the first time. The Company were crying out for more employees and adverts were placed in the local press stating that 300 miners were required who would receive wages of 9s (45p) per shift but the Company's efforts to recruit staff were still being hampered due to the shortage of housing. The company even put on a special Miner's train from Wakefield at shift times to bring in colliers from further a field.

Because of the rapid and successful development of the colliery after the troubles experienced in sinking the shafts, a very relieved and newly knighted Sir Arthur Markham decided to reward his staff and their families with a free day out at the seaside. On Saturday 27th July 1913, 4,000 people were conveyed in 5 trains from Doncaster Station, calling at Carcroft Station *en-route* for Bridlington and Scarborough where everyone was treated to lunch and afternoon tea. The return trains left the resorts at various times in the evening and the last train returned to Doncaster at 4am the following morning, where the site of numerous exhausted day trippers walking back to their homes must have made quite a scene at that time in the morning!

The outbreak of the First World War saw some men leave to join the army but mining was a protected occupation and the government of the day pressed for increasing production to help the war effort. The pit had recorded its first profit in 1913 which had substantially increased in 1914 and during the war years the price of coal rapidly increased. Sir Arthur Markham proudly announced that due to the outrageous prices of coal that were being obtained, in order to help the war effort he would not sell coal at over 15 shillings per ton (75 pence in today's money!). Nevertheless in 1914 a substantial profit was made and Bullcroft Main Collieries Ltd. paid its first dividend of 10% to its shareholding Markham family.

During these years of financial boom, Sir Arthur Markham had secured another coal lease from Earl Fitzwilliam and Doncaster Corporation at Armthorpe. This lease was taken up by Bullcroft Main Collieries in 1915 and it was proposed to develop another pit at Armthorpe. This would be a joint venture between Arthur Markham's Bullcroft Company and Charlie Markham's Staveley Company and each concern put up £150,000. However, as well as the price of coal rapidly increasing so was inflation and the cost of sinking collieries. By 1919, the Armthorpe venture required two more partners and so they persuaded the Hickleton Main Colliery Co. and the Brodsworth Main Colliery Co. to each put in £150,000. The new Markham Main Colliery Co. Ltd. at Armthorpe would be controlled by 4 equal 25% shareholdings and this story is told in the Hatfield & Markham Main booklet in this series.

Bullcroft Colliery from a postcard c1914. The pit is now in full production and the original chimney has been supplemented by a second taller chimney on the right. The Luhrig coal washery and screens building has been completed and a rake of the Company's coal wagons can be seen waiting to be loaded with coal. Careful scrutiny of these private owner wagons reveals that each one features a picture of a bull! – See Page 24. (Photo by James Simonton, issued as a postcard by Doncaster Rotophoto).

Another coal lease that Sir Arthur Markham had secured was also acquired by Bullcroft Main Collieries Ltd. in 1915. This was at Palterton near Bolsover in Derbyshire where a subsidiary colliery, the Ramcroft Colliery Co. Ltd. was formed to develop this small colliery which began production in 1917 employing around 1000 men.

In 1916 Bullcroft Colliery was connected by a two mile branch line to a new railway line that had been built by The Hull & Barnsley & Great Central Joint Railway in order to tap the coal traffic from the various Doncaster area collieries. Bullcroft now had two independent railway outlets and dispatched coal over the new line to the docks at Hull. The other railway line, the West Riding & Grimsby Railway, a joint Great Northern and Great Central Railway project, conveyed Bullcroft coal to Goole Docks.

Sir Arthur Markham died in 1916 at his Nottinghamshire home at Newstead Abbey, the former home of the romantic poet Lord Byron. In recognition of his achievements in the Doncaster Coalfield, the Armthorpe Colliery was named after him in his honour. His brother Charlie Markham took over as Chairman of Bullcroft Main Collieries whilst William Humble was promoted to Managing Director. The new pit manager was Mr T Blunt who had transferred in from Oxcroft Colliery.

During the war years production at Bullcroft had reduced to pre-1914 levels and employment levels had dropped to 2,100 due to the war effort and the effects of enlistment. An important step forward was the linking up of Bullcroft and Brodsworth collieries by an overhead electric cable. Electric power generated at each pit could be fed to the other and it was hoped to extend the cable to Markham Main colliery at Armthorpe to assist with the sinking of that pit after the end of the war.

Following the end of the First World War the owners of Bullcroft Colliery were looking forward to increasing production and profits. However, they were affected by high levels of absenteeism which in 1919 reached 400 men on certain days. This was holding back production from 24,000 tons to 18,000 tons per week. The Markhams has been advocates of the temperance organisation and Charlie Markham blamed the high rates of absence on the fact that a shortage in national beer production caused men to stay away on days when fresh supplies of beer were delivered to Carcroft! The thought of thirsty miners drinking the village dry and eagerly awaiting the delivery of new supplies seems very amusing!

Opposite Page: *Bullcroft Main Colliery depicted on a postcard by an anonymous photographer in 1913 or 1914. Such was the rapid pace in which the colliery developed once coal had been reached, most of the original surface buildings had to be replaced with larger structures within 10 years, including the headgears, chimney and coal preparation plant. The No. 1 headgear has been partially enclosed with a square sectioned steel collar to assist the ventilation of the pit, air entering the colliery through the open downcast No. 2 shaft, passing around the workings and exiting via the upcast No. 1 shaft. (Stan Longley Collection).*

In 1919, five Doncaster Collieries: Bullcroft, Hickleton, Brodsworth, Yorkshire Main and Markham Main each put up £100,000 to form The Doncaster Collieries Association Ltd. (D.C.A.), at the suggestion of Charlie Markham, who not content with being a producer of coal had ambitions to be a great seller of coal. From thereon the D.C.A. would sell all the coal produced from the five collieries above at a commission of 6d per ton. Its profits would be returned as dividends to the five controlling colliery companies which held this money in an undeclared account separate to their own profits. This was much to the annoyance of the miners' leaders who were trying to obtain pay rises when the colliery owners were claiming that profits were down, despite holding a separate account accruing rich dividends from the D.C.A! In the early 1920s the D.C.A. was handling around 5,000,000 tons per year on a 6d a ton commission which generated an income of £125,000 which, after expenses, was returned as healthy dividends to the five owning colliery companies.

At the start of the new decade with increasing output, profits were steadily increasing for Bullcroft Main Collieries Ltd. In 1920 a hefty 15% dividend was paid to the Markham family as controlling shareholders and in 1921 it was announced that a share bonus would be distributed by the capitalisation of reserves of money built up from wartime profits. The sum of £200,000 in undivided profits would be distributed to shareholders by increasing the capital of the company from £600,000 to £800,000.

The 1920s were a boom time for coal production in the Doncaster area and by 1923 output at Bullcroft was approaching 30,000 tons of coal per week and the firm of Simon Carves Ltd. had completed a new 'Baum' washery to process the increased output. In 1922 over 3,000 men were employed and the company was again trying to recruit miners but this was being held back by the shortage of housing. They had built Carcroft New Village before the war and at the same time speculative builders had built numerous terraces in Carcroft and Adwick to privately rent to miners. A new estate would be required to house the extra staff and so the company commissioned the Industrial Housing Association Ltd. to build an area of housing which they named New Skellow. This was largely completed by 1926, the year of the General Strike, when great hardship was experienced by the Bullcroft workforce who had withdrawn their labour.

In 1925, prior to his death, the Bullcroft Chairman, Charlie Markham, sold some of his assets in order to provide an income for his dependents. His engineering company Markham & Co. was sold to the Staveley Coal & Iron Co. Ltd. of which he was also the Chairman. Although unconfirmed, it is possible that he also sold his stake in Bullcroft Main Collieries Ltd. to the Staveley Company at the same time. The controlling stake held by Sir Arthur Markham presumably stayed with his estate and passed to his dependants on his death back in 1916 although this is also unconfirmed.

On 29th June 1926 Charlie Markham died and his place as Chairman was taken by William Humble who had previously been Managing Director. William Humble was a somewhat less controversial man than Arthur and Charlie Markham and seemed to keep his affairs to himself. He lived at Skellow Grange and when he wasn't at the colliery offices, he was involved in the breeding of race horses at the Skellow Grange stables.

After the General Strike the later years of the 1920s are ones of solid progress at Bullcroft as production achieved over 1,000,000 tons of coal per year and the workforce averaged around 2,800-3,000. However, the 1930s saw the country go into depression and each colliery was imposed with a quota system by the government under the Mines Act (1930). This had the effect of limiting coal production and thus preventing the price of coal from collapsing due to over production during the recession. Bullcroft was limited to producing 700,000 tons as part of its annual quota and thus the workforce was reduced to around 2,600 and many employees were laid off.

Despite the drop in production in the 1930s, these were still profitable years for Bullcroft Main Collieries Ltd. and the following profits were recorded:

1930: £94,547, dividend of 10% paid
1931: £56,196, dividend of 3% paid.
1932: £42,317, dividend of 5% paid.
1933: £55,045, dividend of 5% paid.
1934: £63,700, dividend of 6% paid.
1935: £39,067, dividend of 5% paid.
1936: £24,497, dividend of 5% paid.

These figures were very commendable considering the country was in the middle of the Great Depression, although the dividends paid to the shareholders were much lower than those awarded from the earlier years.

An interesting scheme was introduced by Bullcroft Colliery in 1934. Each employee was provided with a free pint of milk at the end of their shift. A surprising safety initiative was the introduction of hard hats to protect the miners' heads from injuries. Up to then miners had not worn hard hats, preferring to wear the traditional flat caps. The company gave each miner the option of renting a hard hat or they could buy one from them at half price!

The Mines Act (1930) had seen the formation of the Coal Mines Reorganisation Committee. The intention was that this organisation would help and encourage the amalgamation of mining companies, thereby increasing their efficiency and productivity which would be helpful during the depression of the 1930s. When the initial response was disappointing the Committee attempted to compulsorily merge colliery companies but with no greater success. However, a number of mine owners saw the benefits of amalgamation and did so voluntarily, and one such scheme saw the merging of the Doncaster coalfield interests belonging to Bullcroft Main Collieries Ltd, Staveley Coal & Iron Co. Ltd and Hickleton Main Colliery Co. Ltd.

On 20th February 1937, The Doncaster Amalgamated Collieries Ltd. (D.A.C.) was formed to take over the operation of Bullcroft, Brodsworth, Firbeck, Hickleton, Markham and Yorkshire Main collieries plus The Doncaster Collieries Association, the selling agency that these collieries controlled. The new concern had a combined capital of £7,750,000. Bullcroft Main Collieries Ltd. was dissolved with the shares exchanged for shares in D.A.C. Ltd. At this time Bullcroft's subsidiary at Ramcroft was sold to the Hardwick Colliery Co. Back in the mid 1920s, the other subsidiary colliery at Oxcroft had been sold and the proposed plan for a colliery at Barnby Dun had been abandoned. The new D.A.C. Head Office would be at The Lodge, South Parade, Doncaster, premises previously used by the Doncaster Collieries Association. Mr William Humble from Bullcroft Main Collieries was appointed as the first Chairman of D.A.C.

At the first annual general meeting of D.A.C, Mr Humble stated that his 6 collieries produced 6,000,000 tons per year and employed 16,000 men. The collieries were capable of producing 10,000,000 tons between them but they were only allowed to run at 60% capacity due to the government's quota system which was still in place. The company owned 6,000 houses and they were all kept in good order by their employees and their families. The following profits were recorded:

1938: £356,538, dividend of 5% paid.
1939: £124,114, no dividend paid.
1940: £289,250, dividend of 4% paid.
1941: Unknown
1942: £382,485, dividend of 5% paid
1943: £463,626, dividend of 5% paid.

William Horsley Humble, Chairman of Bullcroft Main Collieries 1926-1937; and Doncaster Amalgamated Collieries 1937-1947. Following nationalisation, Mr Humble retired to his home at Skellow Grange where he bred race horses and became a notable race horse owner. William Humble followed his father and grandfather into the management side of the coal industry. His Son became a test pilot for the Royal Air Force during the Second World War and his great grand daughter is B.B.C. TV. Presenter Kate Humble. (Colliery Guardian).

During the late 1930s, Doncaster Amalgamated Collieries commenced a programme of modernisation and mechanisation at their collieries in an attempt to increase the efficiency of production. At Bullcroft experiments were made with the introduction of coal cutting equipment and around 1940, the No. 2 shaft the upcast shaft where coal was brought to the surface, was replaced with a reinforced concrete headgear.

During the war years, Bullcroft Colliery lost a lot of its workforce due to enlistment and its output reduced to around 500,000 tons per year, produced by a workforce of 1,500. Many Bevan Boys and Polish refugees worked at the pit at this time. Up to 1943 only the Barnsley Coal Seam had been worked, but from this date the Dunsil Coal Seam was extracted at a depth of 685 yards.

On the 1st January 1947, the mines were nationalised, much to the pleasure of the employees, and the National Coal Board (N.C.B.) took over the management of Bullcroft Colliery from D.A.C. who would receive £6,578,000 for their 6 collieries.

Various improvements were initiated by the N.C.B. at Bullcroft, one of the first being the opening of pithead baths in 1951. Throughout the 1950s and early 1960s production remained more or less constant at around 500,000 tons per year produced by 1,500 employees, similar to that which had been achieved during the Second World War. However, towards the end of the 1960s much of the Barnsley and Dunsil Coal Seams had been extracted from Bullcroft's royalty and production and employment numbers gradually declined. The almost total extraction of the coal within Bullcroft's royalty within 70 years came not as a surprise as the colliery is surrounded by three large pits within a radius of 3 miles, at Askern, Brodsworth and Bentley.

In 1970 an underground connection was made with Brodsworth Colliery which would enable the remaining Bullcroft coal to be brought to the surface at Brodsworth, thus saving the N.C.B. a considerable sum of money. On Monday 27th September 1970 the last shift was worked at Bullcroft Colliery and the remaining 700 men transferred to Brodsworth Colliery the following day.

Demolition of the surface buildings and the filling in of the shafts commenced in the early 1970s and the spoil heap was landscaped by the South Yorkshire County Council in 1974. A small plaque was fixed on a wall near the original entrance to commemorate the pit and a pithead winding wheel was later erected on this site and a small memorial garden was opened. Following demolition of the colliery, the site continued to be used by the N.C.B. as Carcroft Workshops until 1985 when it became an industrial estate. The shafts are presently marked by small concrete pillars which are hidden in the undergrowth near the memorial garden.

Finally, it is often wondered why the colliery was called Bullcroft instead of being named after one of the local villages, i.e. Skellow, Carcroft or Owston. The fact that Bullcroft and Carcroft have the same suffix *croft* is purely coincidental. It seems that the Markham family liked the idea of inventing names by combining the name of a domesticated farm animal with the suffix *croft*. Hence the names for the three collieries that they owned at *Ox*-croft, *Bull*-croft and *Ram*-croft.

Colliery Companies had to provide their own railway wagons to transport their coal across the railway network and many eventually developed fleets of hundreds of these private owner wagons. Most were painted red with black iron work although Bullcroft's differed in design to other collieries as they featured a picture of the white "Bullcroft Bull" that the company used as a logo. Wagon No 288 was part of a fleet of 100 similar wagons purchased in 1912. (The Historical Model Railway Society; Catalogue Number ACA025).

Carcroft New Village & New Skellow

Carcroft New Village from the air c1925 pictured on a postcard published by Aerofilms. The original part of the New Village comprising the oval shaped Markham Avenue, Owston Road & Paxton Avenue, constructed in 1912-3 can be seen towards the top left. The extension built in 1919 forming New Street runs along the bottom and right hand sides of the picture.

Whilst the colliery was undergoing development the company announced that they would construct a new village to house its workforce which would be built to a high standard and therefore prevent the area around the pit becoming an eyesore. A site either side of the lane leading to Owston Hall adjacent to Owston Park was chosen for the building of 300 houses that would form Carcroft New Village. The site was isolated from the old village of Carcroft by fields but connected to it and hence to the pit by Owston Road. Arthur Markham had been involved with the development of Woodlands Model Village at nearby Brodsworth Colliery and although no attempt was made to replicate the more pleasing aspects of Woodlands, the houses of Carcroft New Village were well built and a definite improvement on the standard of housing that most other miners were living in at the time.

Carcroft New Village consisted of a main road which connected the old village of Carcroft with the Owston Hall Lodge on Lodge Road. This road was originally known as Park Lane but was renamed Owston Road after the estate village of Owston. In 1912, houses were built in blocks of 4 along Owston Road & Lodge Road, whilst Markham Avenue was laid out as a loop with a single entrance from Owston Road. Markham Avenue formed a service road to the rear of the properties which faced into a central area of gardens or outwards over fields depending on which side of the circle they were situated. Thus the Markham Avenue houses were built 'back to front' with the back gardens fronting the road with the front gardens behind the houses.

In 1913 Paxton Avenue was built and the houses were laid out in a traditional style with a small front garden and a larger back garden. The Markhams had married into the Paxton family as Arthur and Charlie's mother was the daughter of Joseph Paxton, the famous designer of the Crystal Palace in London and the Chatsworth House landscape gardener.

An unusual scheme was in place at Carcroft New Village where the miners were given the option to make additional payments to their weekly rent in order that eventually they would be able to own their own home leading to an early form of home ownership. Sir Arthur Markham believed that this would have the effect of the employees maintaining their houses to a high standard and having a permanent interest in their locality as they were to eventually become home owners. It is not known how successful this scheme was.

Much closer to the colliery, a group of semi-detached villas was built along the south side of Skellow Road to house pit managers and deputies. These houses were much larger than those of Carcroft New Village and they featured an early form of central heating where hot water from the steam boilers at the pit was pumped through the houses.

At the same time that Bullcroft Main Collieries were building Carcroft New Village, the area was attracting the attention of private builders who erected speculative housing. Although Arthur Markham had stated that he didn't want the Carcroft area to become an eyesore, the 'New Village' consisted of only 300 houses and the unexpected costs incurred in sinking the shafts may have restricted the number of houses he could afford to build. Therefore private builders rushed to complete their houses and this led to poor quality standards of

Above: *Owston Road was originally known as Park Lane. Only the western half has been completed in this postcard from 1912. Note the old 'China Cottage' in the trees on the far right.*
Below: *Taken from a similar viewpoint c1916, the eastern half of the new village has been completed and the trees cut down exposing Owston Hall Lodge at the top of the road. The houses of Carcroft New Village were built to the designs of the architect and builder Benjamin Marson who had recently constructed 304 houses at Highfields for Brodsworth Colliery. (Photographer unknown / Edgar Scrivens).*

workmanship. However, the speculative builders would be able to charge relatively high rents due to the demand for houses.

During 1912 and 1913 private builders constructed rows of terraced housing along Skellow Road, Park Avenue, Queens Road, Askern Road and the lower part of Owston Road, almost surrounding the older village of Carcroft and much nearer to the pit than Carcroft New Village. Many of the old stone built cottages along High Street and Skellow Lane were replaced with brick built shops which serviced the new settlement.

However, a more controversial speculative building scheme was taking place along the road towards Adwick Railway Station, where terraces were built on Bentley Moor Lane, Church Lane, Planet Road, Victoria Road, Edward Road & Adwick Lane. The standards of construction were exceptionally low and the manager of the nearby Askern Colliery described this settlement as "a disgrace to civilisation which they had no intentions of repeating at Askern". Reporters from the Doncaster Gazette were also similarly unimpressed. The problem seemed to stem from a lack of fresh water and sewage connections and in May 1913 it was reported that the tenants were experiencing problems, particularly on Planet Road and Domino Row on Church Lane where they were making holes in the walls to let the sewage flow out of the back yards and the women were walking on bricks through the pools of sewage in order to hang out the washing to dry. The cellars were half filled with a mixture of sewage and water.

Not surprisingly, health conditions in the early days in this area were shocking with high levels of typhoid, diarrhoea and infant mortality and these concerns were discussed at a meeting of Adwick Parish Council in September 1913. Councillor Dr. Ashford drew attention to massive overcrowding in the terraces with many of the houses being home to two or three families. Several of the houses were home to 15 people at a time and there was one house on Domino Row inhabited by 18 people. The council were seeking urban powers which would increase their budget and enable them to construct their own council houses. In the meantime a sewer was constructed along Church Lane. The poor standards of construction probably led to the demolition of the housing between Adwick Station and Carcroft in the 1970s and 1980s.

The outbreak of the First World War brought to a halt plans to build further houses. However other projects were completed during this time and on December 1915 Miss Joy Markham, the daughter of Sir Arthur Markham opened the new Wesleyan Chapel and West Riding schools on Owston Road. The foundation stone for the chapel had been laid earlier that year by Sir Arthur

Markham who had been knighted in 1911. £100 towards the building costs was each given by both the colliery company and Sir Arthur Markham.

Planet Road ran behind Adwick Railway Station and was originally known as Ings Lane and formed part of the controversial speculative housing that was built by private builders and where many of the two up – two down terraces were overcrowded with up to 18 people in each house. Note the Bullcroft pit chimney in the far distance. (Postcard by Edgar Scrivens).

Following the end of the First World War, two further housing schemes were built and opened in 1919. The first was provided by Adwick Urban Council and comprised 65 pairs of semi detached houses built at Skellow consisting of Briar Road, Birch Avenue & Beech Road. The second scheme was constructed by Bullcroft Main Collieries and consisted of an extension to Carcroft New Village where New Street was laid with 150 houses. This scheme cost £30,000 to build and the houses each with 3 bedrooms and in blocks 2 and 4 were erected under the plans of a notable town planner and Liberal MP, Sir Tudor Walters who was an old colleague of Sir Arthur Markham.

By the early 1920s Bullcroft Colliery was looking to further increase their output. Yet there was still a shortage of houses and this was holding back coal production as miners would not work at a pit if there was nowhere to live. This was a factor shared by many of the South Yorkshire collieries at this time and the only answer to the problem would be for several of the colliery companies to combine together to form their own house building company. Thus in 1922 Bullcroft Main Collieries became one of the founder members of The Industrial Housing Association Ltd (I.H.A). Each of the 10 initial members contributed £100,000 into the I.H.A. which between 1922 and 1928 would build 12,000 houses for its member companies under the guidance of Sir Tudor Walters who had worked with Bullcroft before on the New Street development in 1919.

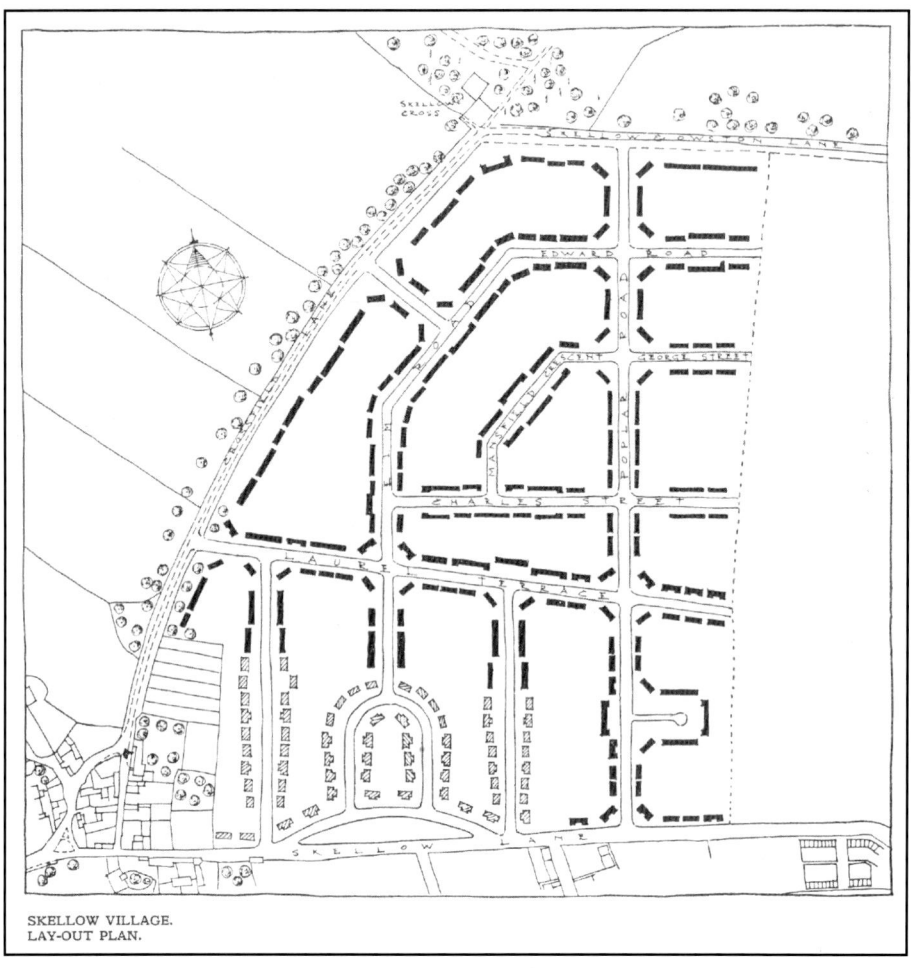

The Industrial Housing Association's plan for New Skellow or Skellow Village as depicted in the book 'The Building of 12,000 houses' by Sir Tudor Walters. The land for Skellow Village was secured from the Davis-Cooke family of Owston Hall. Houses completed by the I.H.A. are shaded black; those constructed in 1919 by Adwick Urban District Council are shown shaded grey.

In 1923 plans were drawn up for an estate of 500 houses which would initially be known as New Skellow in the area between Lodge Road / Crossfield Lane and Skellow Road. Part of this area had been developed as a small housing estate by Adwick Urban District Council in 1919 where the streets were named after trees and shrubs. This theme would be continued for some of the street names of New Skellow, which included Poplar Road, Elm Road & Laurel Terrace. Other streets were named after English Kings, including Charles Street, George Street & Edward Road. The only exception to this plan was Mansfield Crescent, so named because Sir Arthur Markham had previously been Liberal M.P. for the Nottinghamshire town of Mansfield from 1895-1900.

Postcard by Edgar Scrivens of Crossfield Lane looking towards Old Skellow c1928. The newly built Industrial Housing Association houses are on the left whilst Acacia Road would soon be laid out on the right hand side.

The houses built by I.H.A. at New Skellow were built in blocks of 2, 4 and 6 and were built to the highest standards of their day. The plans for New Skellow also included a public house, named the Bullcroft Hotel, which was built on Skellow Road. The south side of Skellow Road was developed as a small shopping area to serve New Skellow. The housing development in this area was largely completed by 1925 but even this didn't stem the demand for houses as Adwick Urban District Council had to build a further housing estate on the north side of

Above: *Children can be seen enjoying the open air paddling pool that was built in the mid 1920s near Mill Lane and this postcard was probably photographed in the summer of 1928. The houses in the distance are on Skellow Road. Today the remains of the paddling pool can still be discerned on the banks of The River Skell to the north of the bridge into the Bridgewater Park housing estate.*
Below: *The south side of Skellow Road was laid out with a shopping parade and the estate was provided with a public house, the Bullcroft Hotel (now demolished). Both views are from postcards published by Edgar Scrivens.*

Crossfield Lane which included Acacia Road. This estate of 120 houses was largely completed by 1930. The development of New Skellow was completed when a new Junior and Secondary Modern school was opened by the West Riding County Council on Lodge Road.

The Mining Industry Act (1920) had seen the establishment of the British Miners Welfare Fund whose purpose was to improve the social well-being, recreation and general conditions in the coalfields of the country. The fund gained its income from a levy of a penny on every ton of coal produced As New Skellow was being constructed it was felt that a Miners Welfare was required and in February the Bullcroft Miners Welfare Committee, using a grant from the Welfare Fund, purchased 10 acres of land off Chestnut Avenue for £1,000 from Mr Davis Cooke. The Miners Welfare Building, Welfare Park and Recreation Grounds cost £3,000 paid for by a further grant, and were opened by Mr William Humble on Saturday 31st January 1925. Around this time an open air paddling pool was constructed by damming the River Skell near Mill Lane in the old village of Skellow.

In the early 1950s, the Carcroft and Skellow area was photographed by James Simonton & Sons in order to produce a series of commercial postcards which bear the firm's initials J. S .& S. The Carcroft Miners Welfare Hall was opened by William Humble in 1925. In the 1990s the Welfare Hall suffered a fire and had to be demolished. However, the structure was replaced with a new community building known as the Bullcroft Memorial Hall

Carcroft High Street photographed by Edgar Scrivens in 1928. **Above:** *The cinema opened in 1924 and was demolished in the early 1990s to make way for a supermarket. On the left the Camplejohns motorbus has just arrived from Doncaster. Camplejohns were taken over by The Yorkshire Traction Bus Company in the early 1930s. Compare this view with the illustration on Page 5. (Paul Fox Collection).* **Below:** *Carcroft High Street from Galleon's Corner looking towards Bullcroft Colliery with the replacement chimney prominent. By the 1920s Carcroft High Street had developed into a small shopping centre to serve the new colliery settlement.*

The Bullcroft Hotel opened in 1925 as part of the development of New Skellow by the Industrial Housing Association, who leased the building to John Smith's Tadcaster Breweries. The Markham Brothers had been keen believers in the temperance movement but their influence within Bullcroft Main Collieries had ceased with their death and, as it is well known that mining is thirsty work, by the 1920s several Working Men's Clubs had become established in the area. The new management of Bullcroft Main Collieries decided that their efforts would be more financially productive by opening their own licensed establishment and leasing it to a brewery - as the saying goes "if you can't beat 'em, join 'em"! Following the retraction in the public house trade due to various factors, the Bullcroft Hotel closed in 2006 and was subsequently demolished and the site used to construct a block of flats.

In the 1920s further developments occurred in the old village of Carcroft when in 1924 a large cinema called the Carcroft Picture House was opened on High Street. Prior to this the people of Carcroft had been served by the New Empire Cinema which had opened in 1912 on Church Lane near Adwick Railway Station. In 1925 the Moon Inn closed and moved from High Street to new purpose built premises at the junction of High Street and Skellow Road and reopened as The New Moon. Back in 1919 there had been proposals to extend the Doncaster Corporation Trams to Carcroft but this scheme was replaced with a motor bus service in 1922. Yorkshire Traction buses operated to Barnsley in one direction and to Woodlands tram terminus in the other direction where connections were made for Doncaster.

During the 1930s, the country went into depression and the pit was on a reduced output due to the quota system and developments at Carcroft and Skellow were few and far between. This continued through the 1940s during the Second World War. In the 1950s the fields between New Skellow and Carcroft New Village were converted into a housing estate by the Doncaster Rural Council and Chestnut Avenue, Milton Road and Grasmere Roads were laid out and housing was also built along the continuations of Charles Street, George Street and Edward Road. Further housing developments have seen the linking up of the once individual settlements of Five Lane Ends by the A1, Old Skellow, New Skellow, Carcroft & Carcroft New Village into a continuous urban area nearly two miles long.

Following the closure of Bullcroft Colliery the N.C.B. transferred the ownership of New Skellow and Carcroft New Village to Doncaster Council. People in the area now work at many of the surrounding industrial estates as well as commuting to Doncaster and Leeds following the opening of a successful park and ride scheme at Adwick Railway Station.

Glossary

Barnsley Coal Seam
A seam of coal up to 10 feet thick within the Coal Measures of South Yorkshire which is only found at the surface near the town of Barnsley.

Bunker
A large container used for the storage of coal before the coal can be treated in the screens and washery of a coal preparation plant.

Cage
Steel structure used to transport men or coal filled tubs up and down the shafts. Some cages had two decks. The cage was attached by a steel rope to the winding engine.

Coal Measures
A thick sequence of rocks and strata which consists of sandstones, shales, clays and coal seams. The coal measures of Yorkshire contain around 30 different coal seams.

Coal Preparation Plant.
A building where the treatment of coal is undertaken prior to dispatch, usually containing screens, washery and a conveyor leading to a rapid loading bunker.

Coalfield (Exposed & Concealed)
An area of land above coal measure rocks. A coalfield may be "exposed", i.e. the coal measures are found at the surface, or "concealed" where they are hidden at greater depths beneath younger rocks. Doncaster is situated on a concealed coalfield where the coal measures are buried beneath Magnesian Limestone and Bunter Sandstones.

Drift
A sloping tunnel connecting coal seams to the base of the shafts or to the surface.

Fault
A geological fracture resulting from the upward or downward movement of the strata on either side.

Gob
The area left following removal of a coal seam. It is supported with waste material or allowed to collapse in a controlled way.

Headgear
A structure of wooden, steel lattice or reinforced concrete construction situated above the shafts and used to support the winding wheel.

Longwall Mining
A method of coal working in which coal is mined from a long coal face. The coal face connects two tunnels which lead back to the base of the shafts. The coalface thus advances away from the shafts leaving an area of gob behind. This method was later replaced by retreat mining.

Main
A suffix used mainly in South Yorkshire to denote those collieries which mined the largest or main seam from the coal measures, i.e. the Barnsley Seam

Pillar and Stall Mining
A method of coal working where coal was extracted from areas known as stalls leaving pillars of coal to support the surface. Largely replaced with longwall mining due to the advance in technology in the 19th Century.

Pit
A local term for a coal mine or colliery

Rapid Loading Bunker
A large bunker containing many tons of coal which is dropped into railway wagons passing beneath the structure.

Retreat Mining
The most economical method in mining in which roadways are driven out to the extremity of the royalty to where a coal face can then be worked back towards the shaft bottom. Largely superseded longwall mining in the 1950s/1960s.

Roadways
Underground tunnels leading from the bottom of the shaft to the coal faces.

Royalty
An area of land beneath which coal can be extracted by paying a fee or royalty on every ton produced to the landowner.

Screens
A building containing numerous devices for sorting individual lumps of coal by size or weight

Shafts
A vertical tunnel from the surface to the coal seam through which the coal is extracted and men and materials can access the workings. Following a mining disaster at Hartley Colliery in Durham each colliery was required to have two shafts, downcast and upcast, to aid escape in the event of an accident. Air was pumped through the downcast shaft to ventilate the workings and then drawn out of the colliery via the upcast shaft.

Shaft Pillar
A large area of coal left intact in order to support the colliery's surface buildings and thus protect them from the effects of subsidence. Some coal was removed from the shaft pillar to form roadways or tunnels to access the underground workings.

Sinking
The process of tunnelling vertically downwards from the surface to the coal seam in order to construct a shaft, usually undertaken by workers called sinkers who specialised in this highly skilled but dangerous work.

Skip Winding
A method of winding coal up a shaft by the use of a large capacity metal container or skip. A more economical way of transport than that previously used when individual coal filled tubs were brought to the surface in a cage.

Tubbing
A waterproof casing, usually of iron, inserted into a shaft as it was sunk in order to keep back water and soft sediments.

Tubs
Small wagons used to transport coal underground.

Washery
A surface plant for dealing with the cleaning and washing of coal

Winding Engine
Engine, initially steam driven but later powered by electricity, used to raise the cages up and down the shafts.

Bibliography

Barnett, A L (1984). *The Railways of the South Yorkshire Coalfield from 1880.* RCTS Publishing, Devon.

Colliery Guardian (1927). *The Colliery Year Book & Coal Trades Directory.* Louis Cassier Publishing, London.

Doncaster Amalgamated Collieries Limited (1944). A Souvenir Brochure published on the occasion of the visit of the delegation of American Mining Engineers.

Gould S & Ayris I (1995). *Colliery Landscapes. An aerial survey of the deep-mined coal industry in England.* English Heritage / Billington Press Ltd, London.

Hill, Alan (2001). *The South Yorkshire Coalfield, a history and development.* Tempus Publishing, Stroud.

Markham, Violet (1956). *Friendship's Harvest.* The Stellar Press, Barnet, Herts.

Thornes, Robin (1994). *Images of Industry: Coal.* Royal Commission on the historical monuments of England, Swindon.

Walters, Sir J Tudor (1927). *The Building of twelve thousand houses.* Ernest Benn Publishing Ltd, London.

Watts, A J (1998). *Private Owner Wagons from the Ince Waggon & Ironworks Co.* The Historical Model Railway Society

MOTHER'S RUIN

A Sheffield Childhood

Walt Palmer

A People's History of Yorkshire

Yorkshire Art Circus
1988

Published by Yorkshire Art Circus
13-15 Sagar Street
Castleford
West Yorkshire
WF10 1AG

© Walt Palmer 1988
Cover design by Wayne Clarida

Yorkshire Art Circus has made every effort to trace the photographer of the cover photograph, but has been unable to do so. Anyone recognising the photograph should contact Yorkshire Art Circus at the above address as soon as possible.

Typeset by Print Assist, Castleford.
Printed by F.M. Repro, 5 North Road, Ravensthorpe
Dewsbury, West Yorkshire

ISBN 0 947780 54 8

Yorkshire Art Circus is grateful for support from Yorkshire Arts

Yorkshire Art Circus has developed a unique approach to oral history. Taking an individual life as a focus, we combine different forms of expression; for example, writing, performance, painting, photography and bannermaking. Yorkshire Art Circus projects have successfully toured community centres, colleges, galleries, clubs, galas and art centres. For details of our programme of performances, exhibitions, conferences and workshops, please contact the address above.

All the people below have helped to make this project possible:

Christine Walker
Evelyn Haythorne
Rachel Van Riel
Phil Wildin
Margaret Edwards

Olive Fowler
Edwin Harmer
Joan Thornton
Beryl Palmer
Wayne Clarida

To my mother and father for giving me a life to live, and to my wife, family and friends for their constant encouragement.

CITY OF SHEFFIELD EDUCATION COMMITTEE.
Impress School Stamp here.

[S.M. Form 415]

REPORT on the work of **Walter Palmer** Standard **JIa**
for **Year** ended **25 July** 19**46**.

Parents are requested to examine carefully and sign the following Report so that their children may feel they take a deep interest in the work of the School.

SUBJECT	Maximum No. of Marks possible	MARKS EARNED	REPORT
READING	10	7	
WRITING	10	9	
ARITHMETIC—Mental	10	4	
Written	30	30	
ENGLISH (a) Composition	10	8	
(b) Grammar and English Exercises	10	9	
(c) Spelling	10	9½	Walter has done a good
(d) Recitation	10	8	year's work and made
(e) Literature			satisfactory progress. He
GEOGRAPHY	10	10	is a hard worker and is
HISTORY	10	10	very neat and painstaking
SCIENCE—Nature Study	10	10	in all he does.
General Elementary			
ART (including Drawing):—	10	6	
(a) Line and Colour			
(b) Geometrical Drawing			
(c) Technical Drawing			
(d) Design			
MUSIC	10	6	
PHYSICAL TRAINING	10	7	
CRAFTWORK (a) Wood			
(b) Metal			
(c) Needlecraft			
(d) Housecraft			
(e) Other Crafts	10	7	
TOTAL	170	140½	

Position in Class **8**   Number in Class **55**
Attendance possible **385**   Times Absent **6**   Times Late **—**
Conduct and General Remarks **Walter's conduct is good and he is interested in all his lessons He is always neat and tidy in himself**

B. Riley .... Class Teacher.
F. BAILEY .... Head Teacher.
Parent's Signature **A. Palmer**   **W. Palmer**

A Sheffield Childhood

Eleanor Street was a steep cobbled stretch that started at the top of Phillimore Road and ran down past the brick works to the bottom of Darnall Road. In winter, sledging on that stretch was better and faster than the Cresta Run. All sorts of weird and wonderful designs of homemade sledges would appear with the first snow flakes. The main design problems were weight for momentum and speed, and size for seating capacity. Sledge irons or runners were no problem; they were turned out in their hundreds at the steelworks where most of our dads worked. Dad made Herbert and me a sledge each. We watched him sawing the wood, assembling it with nails and rounding the corners. The sledge irons were made from half inch, square steel. The ends had been formed in the steel forge with sharp points enabling them to be driven into the underside of the sledge by various methods. Dad's technique was to heat them in the fire at home until, glowing red hot, they were burned into the wood amid clouds of smoke.

Roads weren't salted in those days and, consequently, the snow lay longer and because of the lack of traffic, it was cleaner. The slow thaws in the day and the freezings at night produced ideal sledging tracks on any sloping road. Ours was Eleanor Street. After tea we put on our clothes and, pulling the heavy sledges behind us, made our way to the top of the road. The snow glistened under the yellow light from the gas lamps and at the start of the track we could see large groups gathering with their sledges. The first run down always needed a lot of nerve as each returning traveller bragged and exaggerated in high excited voices how fast the snow was, "Tons faster than last night!" Eventually, daring overcame fear and with a cautious push the sledge gathered speed and the rush of icy wind tore at red and stinging faces. Chapped, freezing hands held on to the guiding rope for dear life. The wind and frost found their way through our holed, wet gloves causing hot aches to set in. But the thrill was the thing and after one or two runs, confidence at its height, we literally ran back up to the start to go careering down once more. We tried belly flops to gain more speed. Some lay full length and took their younger brothers or sisters, perched on their backs, down to the giddy bottom amid much screaming and yelling.

Someone brought an Anderson Shelter section on to the track. A giant sledge! Parking our sledges at the side of the road we prepared for this new thrill. As it was launched, fifteen foolhardy souls jumped on board. The speed was fantastic, the corrugated folds offering hardly any resistance to the glassy snow. Clutching each other, for that was all there was to hold, we sped down shedding passengers at every yard. Suddenly I lost my footing and found myself sitting dazed in the snow. The crazy sledge carried on down, its back end clear of the track by some two feet as more and more of its load was shed. Nearing the bottom at breakneck speed, the curved metal, now rocking unsteadily, suddenly somersaulted, throwing the three remaining passengers in a great arc. One held on, a fatal decision, for as the shelter section crashed down that brave soul said goodbye to his little finger, staining the snow a bright red.

My brother Herbert was a great sledger. He was frightened of nothing. The faster the better, was his motto. He never put his feet down but steered by body weight alone — this recklessness proved his undoing. At the top a race was organised and we all lined up sitting astride our machines. It had been agreed we all should sit, as some were brilliant belly floppers, my brother included. The shout "Go!" rang out and we were off. Down we sped, our faces set in determination. To my surprise, I was up with the leaders. It was then I saw, far down the track, a dark circular patch which was set in the snow. We saw it every time we flew down and avoided it: it was a sewer manhole cover. No snow settled on it due to the warmth from below. This time, because of the crowding on the track, no-one could guide with any measure of room. Whoever was heading for it would inevitably be thrown off as metal hit metal. Suddenly Herbert wasn't to be seen. A piercing scream rent the air. I swerved my sledge, ground to a halt, and looked back. My brother was writhing in the snow, yelling, while his sledge slewed to a halt, upside down in the side of the road. A man was slipping and sliding towards him. I raced to him feeling frightened. The snow had great patches of blood in it. Herbert lay on his stomach, his short trousers slashed, exposing his ripped bare bottom. Blood flowed everywhere. The man picked him up as though he was a feather.

"Where do you live, son?" he asked.

"He's me brother mester...Coleford Road."

"Right son, fetch his sledge. I'll take him home."

I gathered his sledge, put it across mine, and turned to follow. The man had already disappeared around the top of the road and when I rounded it, I saw him turning down our entry. I was frightened of what mum and dad would say as I slowly turned into the yard. I dumped the sledges unceremoniously by the bin. In the house, pandemonium.

"Who did it son?" demanded my dad.

"Nobody dad." said Herbert.

"I'll kill 'em!" exclaimed dad.

"Shut up Walt," said mum, "and fetch some water and towels."

"What's tha know Walter?" dad asked me.

"He come off his sledge on a manhole cover, dad."

"Well how's he ripped his arse then?"

"It was t'sledge iron, dad," said Herbert. 'Sledge stopped — I carried on. Sledge iron were sticking up through t'burn hole."

"Tha what? I'll kill that sledge!"

Off he flew into the yard. Silence, followed by banging and crashing and dad's muffled curses, resulting in two demolished sledges. In he came, sweating.

"And don't either of you go on a sledge again."

Mum bathed Herbert's considerable wound but obviously bandaging it was impossible. Next day they went to the hospital, and for months after.

The following year dad built us two more sledges.

*

Our house at Coleford Road was in the middle of a long terrace, before a bomb considerably shortened it. After that we were much nearer the end, there being only Thompsons and Brighams before the rubble. Each two houses shared a common yard at the rear, access was gained down the entry. In the yard, with a sloping, slated roof, was the lavatory.

The back door led into the kitchen and a door from that led into the back room in which we lived, ate, argued and laughed. The front room was never used, simply because mum and dad couldn't afford to furnish it. However, up at the window that faced the street a spotless net curtain always hung. Mum was house proud.

Our bedroom was upstairs over the kitchen and the sloping lavatory roof came up to our window. The bedroom walls were painted with deep blue limewash called distemper. A broken chair was our wardrobe and there was a piece of coconut matting on the floor. Our bed was always cold. In winter dad piled his coats and working overcoat on the bed for us. They smelled faintly of engineering oil from the works. On very cold nights he'd wrap the oven plate in a scorched blanket, put it in the bed and we'd climb in. To put our feet on that square of warmth was sheer luxury. When we were safely tucked up, dad took the plate and put it in their bed to use what heat was left. Upstairs frightened me. There was never any lighting up there.

On Saturday, mum cleaned the house thoroughly from top to bottom. We were not allowed in when this happened, no matter the weather or time of year. Mum wasn't cruel, just heart-broken. Sometimes we'd watch her, unobserved, through the back window as she polished the lino on hands and knees using Mansion Polish. She cried quietly to herself. At our age we didn't understand about poverty and, anyway, there were plenty of tears about every day. If we fell and grazed our knees or hands, if we were hit by a stone, or if we were bullied, it was all part of the day.

At twelve o'clock we could go into the kitchen and when my brother brought the chips we had our dinner. Chips and bread and margarine, cut like doorsteps. After, we'd run to the 'Penny Rush' at the Darnall 'Bug Hut', picking up the gang on the way, to watch *The Three Stooges*, *Johnny 'Mac' Brown*, *Flash Gordon* and *Zorro* films. They were all our heroes.

The cellar was a dark, fearsome place. The stone steps led down from a door off the back room. At the bottom was a bend to the left. That's what terrified me — the bend. Always, when forced to fetch coal from down there, I dreaded reaching the bend and what lurked around the corner. I'd shout, all the way down, to my mother, giving her a running commentary of where I was and what I was doing. If she didn't answer at every sentence end, I'd shout, "Mam! Mam! Can you hear me?" and stand until she answered.

"I'm round t'bend, mam."

"Mam, what are you doing?"

"I can see t'coal, mam."

"I'm just fillin t'bucket."
"Mam, what you doing now?"
"I'm on my way back, mam."
"Here I come, mam."

I'd take those stone steps two at a time, flying up to the top and into the room, mum and daylight. I once fell down the cellar steps. The bulb had blown, it was dark at the top. I missed my footing and plunged headlong down towards the pitch-black bend. I lay at the bottom screaming, I was petrified. After what seemed an age, but must have been only a few seconds, mum's arms wrapped around me and I was carried back up. She played hell with me and at the same time loved me better.

Running errands I didn't like, so running errands was done literally running. Come to think of it, I ran everywhere. I loved the speed, and swerving was marvellous! Dad nicknamed me 'Dash', a name that stuck until I was well into my twenties. Mum sent me for bread to the bottom corner shop. Her parting words were always, "And leave the corners on!" On the way back, however, the smell from the warm bread proved irresistible and I nibbled the four corners. It meant a clip round the ears if I wasn't quick, but it was worth it.

*

Directly across from our house stood the vicarage, a very grand, square-built, stone building. It stood in its own grounds and was surrounded by a stone wall topped with wrought iron fencing. It was one of the few properties that still sported its fancy fencing, the others in the area having been stripped for metal to help in the war effort. The vicar, a German, was called Mr Frieze. One night, he and my father were standing outside the vicarage. The sirens had sounded. It may seem strange that they were out of doors during an air raid but people had soon adjusted to the nightly events. In the distance, they could hear the sound of an approaching Doodle Bug. Living near the steel works, quite a few came our way. As it passed directly overhead, the rocket motor cut out and it started its descent in an eerie silence. There was a pause then a terrific explosion which sheared away our chimney pots.

Mr Frieze turned to dad and said, quite casually, "Bloody hell, Walt, that was close."

This matter of fact remark made with a German accent, by a man of the cloth, caused dad to collapse with laughter and they both stood in the street and howled.

Dad got on well with the vicar, unusual really because dad was a big drinker and not at all a churchgoer. He never interfered with mother sending us to church though. Indeed, we were very involved with St Alban's; in the choir, the cubs and, later, the scouts.

*

Playing under the 'flat part' was great fun; the 'flat part' was the collapsed roof of a church next to Mr Frieze's vicarage. A bomb had demolished it and left all sorts of tunnels and holes under the ruins. We had a gang meeting place under there. In our gang was my brother Herbert, my cousins, Barry and Margaret, Rosie Bacon, and the three Thompson lads. Things happened under the ruins that would have curled our parents' hair.

Another of the hundreds of places we played was on the ruins of the fifteen houses that were bombed. We'd hunt amongst the rubble for pennies and halfpennies from the shattered gas meters. We found quite a lot but over a period of time they got scarce as more and more people tumbled to our secret. When the gang from the top of Coleford Road got to know, the game was up, we couldn't get a look in. Anyway, we'd had the bulk and with the money we bought carrots and potatoes from the greengrocer's shop at the top of Jubilee Street. Back in our den, under the 'flat part', we roasted them, in a fashion. The queue for the lone, smoky flame was always impatient, so the yardstick was if they were burnt on the outside and warmed through, they were done. With eyes running and red, we sat gnawing our way through raw, burnt spuds, peering through the acrid smoke that issued from the smouldering carpet on the fire and awaiting Alan's return from the static water tank with a bucketful of bright yellow clay.

Reaching the den, Alan placed the heavy bucket to the ground and made to pull back the linoleum that sealed the door. To his annoyance he found it secured from within.

"Let me in!" he yelled.

"Who's there? Friend or foe?"

"What do you mean, friend or foe? It's me, Alan, with the clay."

There was a pause, then the voice said, "How do we know it's you? It could be an invader. What's the password?"

Alan kicked at the linoleum. "I don't know, do I? I didn't know we had a password today."

"Well we do, what is it?"

"Search me!"

"No, that's not it."

"I know that's not it," Alan said irritably, "Now come on, stop larking about! It's raining out here you know, I'm soaked!"

"Prove you are Alan," the voice said.

Alan's mouth tightened. He felt his blood boil. "Look, if you don't let me in I'll take the clay away." Silence. "I mean it," Alan said, "I'm going. I'm going now. I'm off! Bugger you lot!"

Suddenly the voice said, "Are you with yourself?"

"Of course I'm with myself! Nobody else would be daft enough to stand out here in this rain, would they?"

"You could be a prisoner, and they could be making you say that," the voice answered.

"Look if you don't believe me, come out here and look for yourself."

"What? And get took prisoner as well? Not likely!"

"But there's only me here!" Alan said desperately.

"Prove it."

"How can I prove it, if you won't come outside?"

Impasse.

"Well, I'm going home," Alan said miserably, "I'm fed up, and I'm wet, and I'm taking the clay with me." He turned, stamped his feet on the spot a dozen times, then stood perfectly still. After a pause Enoch said, "Have you gone?"

Silence.

"Alan. Have you gone?"

Silence.

"We were only kidding! We know you haven't gone. Have you gone?"

Silence.

"He's gone," Enoch told the rest of the gang who were all squashed inside, sworn to silence.

"I bet he hasn't," Rosie whispered, "He's kidding us so that we'll open up."

"Alan," Enoch called through the linoleum, "Are you there? If you speak to us, we'll let you in. Alan?"

Silence.

"See. He has gone," Margaret whispered.

Alan silently skirted the mound of broken bricks that was the den. He was smiling and his eyes glittered. He reached the drain pipe that stuck up from the mound which acted as the chimney to the inefficient fire within. Reaching into the bucket he scooped a handful of clay out and carefully sealed the pipe's opening, then quietly he tiptoed back to the entrance.

He smiled as he heard the first cough from within. This was followed by another, then another. Soon the interior sounded like the steelworks' chest clinic on a very bad day. The linoleum trembled, then bulged, and finally burst as the gang poured out, gasping for fresh air. Alan stood laughing as we stumbled about, rubbing our stinging eyes and coughing.

"You burk! You big burk!" Rosie fumed. "That wasn't clever, blocking the chimberley. We could have died in there, then you'd have been sorry."

Alan continued to laugh as Enoch stumbled and fell on to a heap of wet house bricks.

"Serves you right for not letting me in." he answered.

Eventually, taking great gulps of fresh air, we cleared our lungs and calmed down.

"Hey, it's stopped raining," Herbert said looking into the grey sky. "Great!"

"Let's take the cover off the den," Brian suggested, and together we threw the linoleum to one side, revealing the den's interior.

A narrow shaft of bright yellow sunlight burst from the clouds, raked across the ruins, lit the gang for a few seconds, then raced on over the rooftops and into the distance.

"It's brightening up, we'll be able to make the winter warmers outside," Rosie said.

We always made winter warmers when winter came. We went down to the static water tank, next to the vicarage, to gather the yellow, sticky clay from the sides of the slimy water. The clay was patted and flattened until it was formed into a hollow box the size of half a house brick. Two holes were pushed through the sides and a lid made to fit the top. When the clay was hard we found dry sticks and grass and soon had a small fire burning inside. To hold those powdery boxes between our hands when it was freezing was grand. Eventually they'd crack or break from the heat but replacements were easy to make.

Various refinements to the basic box were tried but none ever bettered the original. Another winter warmer we made was more fun and spectacular. We'd forage empty tin cans out of the dust bin and punch them full of holes with the aid of a six inch nail and a stone. A looped length of strong wire was attached to the tin then we put paper, sticks and tiny pieces of coal into it. Once this was lit and the sticks burning we swung the tin round and round causing the fire to burn brightly. Presently the tin started to glow red hot and each one of us would take great pride in tending his or her own fire, keeping them alive for hours until it was time for bed, when the tins were relegated to the back garden. Some of us would go out on the street and, in a grand gesture, swing and swing them; then, letting go, watch them arc into the black sky and finally crash onto the cobblestones, spilling their contents out to die in the cold air.

Some time later, as we sat around the blaze fashioning the clay boxes, Herbert said "The King and Queen are coming to visit our town, me dad says."

"What for?" Enoch asked. "Nothing exciting happens in our town. Just bombing every night and people evacuating themselves all over the place. I wouldn't come here, not if I was the King and Queen. I'd go to...er...er...I'd go to the seaside or...er...London."

"They come from London, burk," Rosie said with a sneer. "That's where they live, London. Not much point in visiting where you live is there?"

"Well, the seaside then," Enoch said.

"Everything is shut at the seaside. Don't forget it's winter, there would be no rides to go on and the sea would be too cold for them to have a paddle. Expect that's why they've come to our town — for a warm in the steelworks," Brian informed everybody.

Rosie nodded her head in agreement at this wise statement.

"My mam is hanging a bun tin outside our bedroom window in case they come up our street," Herbert told the members. "She always hangs a bun tin out. It shows respect and loyalty to our King and Queen, she says."

"Why a bun tin?" Enoch asked.

"Don't know, suppose it's to show that we cook for ourselves and are healthy and ready to defend our country if Hitler decides to come."

"Can't see them wanting to come up our street," Margaret sniffed.

"They could do," Brian defended. "We've got some good ruins to look at. Look at all these," he gestured.

"They don't look at ordinary ruins like these, they go with the Lord Mayor. I bet he shows them better ones than these. I bet the Lord Mayor knows where all the best ruins are in our town."

"Me dad calls me grandma an old ruin to me mother; it dun't half make her mad," Rosie said.

We all giggled.

"Perhaps yer dad will stick yer grandma on a box and they'll come and look at her, then," Enoch laughed.

"And this, your Highness is the best ruin in all the town. I've saved her until last for you to look at — Rosie's grandma," Herbert announced.

The gang laughed. Rosie didn't.

"And they will unveil her," Enoch added.

"And she'll have no pegs in," Alan laughed.

"And the King will cut her apron string and declare her open," Brian screamed.

Rosie sat fuming as the gang rolled about laughing. "Yer daft, you lot," she said in disgust.

"We might be daft," Enoch laughed, "but we haven't got a ruined grandma, have we?"

Rosie turned away and began to sulk. Eventually we grew quiet and continued our work with the winter warmers.

"They must get fed up sometimes though," Margaret said as she fashioned the lid to her box.

"Who gets fed up?" I wanted to know.

"The King and Queen. They must get fed up looking at ruins all day. And shaking hands with everybody."

"They don't shake hands with everybody," Herbert said knowledgeably. "They have a list. They are only allowed to shake hands with important people and people with piles of money. If yer not on the list you don't get a hand shake. You might get a smile but not a hand shake. They're told whose hand is worth shaking and whose isn't beforehand, in the Town Hall, the Lord Mayor tells 'em that. And off they go shaking and smiling to all them on the list. It's called "port of call", is that."

"The Lord Mayor's wife always wears a fur coat, dun't she?" Alan said. When she came to our school to watch us do gas mask practice, she had one on then. They must be dead rich him and her."

"And she always smells nice."

"And she's got red finger nails."

"And she's got her own teeth."

Yes, you're right. They must be dead rich," agreed Herbert. I bet they get more than their fair share of handshakes at King visiting times."

We sat and pondered the injustice of this and wished somehow we could make our own mothers rich enough to get a handshake and some scent instead of just hanging a bun tin from the bedroom window and offering to go four rounds with Hitler.

"When are they coming?" Enoch asked.

"Don't know. They keep that a secret," Herbert answered. "I mean, if Hitler got to know, well knowing him, he'd say, 'Right men, der King and Queen of England are going to see some ruins that we've made. Tell Hans to go and bomb them again tomorrow.' Imagine what would happen then! There wouldn't be much handshaking going off would there? They'd have to go in an air raid shelter and miss their dinner at the Cutlers' Hall."

Enoch nodded an understanding.

"They must be dead brave," Rosie said, "I mean everywhere they go they're in danger from Hitler, aren't they? He's just dying to bomb them. If it was me, I'd change me name to something else and wear ordinary clothes, not crowns and things, they're a dead give away, aren't they? I bet you can see a crown from miles up in a bomber. If I was the King's wife I'd mek him paint it black. They wouldn't see it then, would they?

"That's a good idea," Enoch said, surprising all the gang.

Enoch was notorious for never agreeing with Rosie. Rosie looked at Enoch with disbelief written on her face. Enoch unconcernedly returned to his winter warmer and carefully pushed his thumb through the side of the box to create the blowing hole.

"Mine's nearly finished," he said.

"I can't get me lid to fit properly," Margaret complained.

No-one took any notice and she continued to squeeze the clay, becoming more and more frustrated.

"Our Queen always wears lovely clothes dun't she?" said Rosie, "She must have a frock for every day of the week, and hats to match."

"I bet it costs our King a bob or two to keep her togged out," Margaret said as she endeavoured to control the wayward clay.

"I wouldn't stand for it," said Enoch. "I wouldn't spend all me money, if I had any, on women's clothes. Not even if I was married to a Queen."

Rosie glared across at him. The truce was over. They were once more in disagreement. Somehow it felt more comfortable for them both.

Suddenly Barry said, "Does Germany have a King and Queen?"

"Shouldn't think so," Brian replied. "If they did have, Hitler's got their job now. He's probably sold their crowns and thrones to the German rag-and-bone man for scrap. I bet that's where he's got all the money to buy bombs from."

"Fancy him doing that!" Herbert exclaimed. "Our King wouldn't stand for that if Mr Churchill tried to do the same. The King would have him in his office and tell him straight. 'Look here Mr Churchill,' he'd say. 'Look, I'll let you have the job of winning the war for us, you can tell all my soldiers and sailors what to do but don't think you are getting my job off me or else there'll be trouble! And Mr Churchill would bow and say, 'I won't tek your job your Highness, you're the best King I know, and everybody at the ruins likes you.' And the King and Queen would smile at him and say, 'Thank you Mr Churchill, you can go now and start winning the war from Hitler. Remember us to your wife Winnie.' And Mr Churchill would smile, put two fingers up at them, and say 'Thank you, your Highnesses,' and he'd go back to his office of war and get a drink out of his war cabinet."

After this outburst of patriotism Herbert sat down on his house brick once again and completed his winter warmer, whilst the rest of the gang digested his speech. No-one found a flaw in it and so we all continued to put the finishing touches to our boxes in silence.

Some time later, when all the boxes had been placed around the fire to dry, Barry said, "Do you think the King made winter warmers when he was our size?"

"Shouldn't think so. Can't see him being allowed to drag

buckets of clay into their house, I bet it's ever so posh."

"That's right," Rosie interrupted. It was Enoch's turn to be surprised at this sudden agreement. "They miss a lot of fun out of life being royal, me mam says. They're not allowed to get mucky like we are, or play in a gang. They have to sit around all day keeping clean and being royal. If he wants a winter warmer, I expect he sends out for one. Not much fun in that! It's better to make your own any day. I mean, he might get a duff one that doesn't work. Then he'd have to walk around his house with cold hands all winter. That would mek him mad, I bet."

"He doesn't live in a house," Margaret said quietly, "he lives in a palace, a palace is a lot bigger than a house."

Rosie spun on her. "Well, whatever he lives in, he'll still have cold hands won't he? No, I still say it's better to mek your own winter warmers. It's more reliable." The gang all nodded and glanced with pride at their craft as it slowly dried.

"Fancy not being able to mek a winter warmer," said Herbert. "I thought everybody knew how to mek a winter warmer."

Suddenly there was a crack, Herbert's box split open and then fell to pieces.

Enoch glanced at the shattered remains, sniffed, looked at Herbert, and said, 'So did I.'

*

During the war, dad was sent away to work on the docks at Barrow-in-Furness. I don't remember him going but remember him reappearing one night. We stood around the table in the back room. He hoisted his cardboard suitcase onto the plush cloth and after rummaging about in it, brought out some blue sugar bags. He gave one to Herbert and one to me. We opened them quickly and inside were hundreds of peanuts still in their shells. We'd never seen peanuts. We stood in our pyjamas around the Yorkshire range and listened as he told us how he'd shovelled millions of peanuts out of the holds of ships, and how he'd smuggled the two bags past the gate guard especially for us. He held my mum's hand as he talked, the first time I'd seen him do that. She was smiling and looking lovely.

We went to bed with our peanuts clutched in our arms and ate them under the covers till Herbert nearly choked on one. We fell asleep whispering and laughing. The more we whispered, the more we laughed, until we were in hysterics.

I remember the bombing; being pulled from my bed in the middle of the night and carried downstairs in my siren suit. The stairs were very steep and narrow with a door to one side at the bottom, opening into the back room. I felt dad's rough, stubbly, unshaven chin as he carried me down and out through the yard into the air raid shelter he had dug in the tiny back garden.

The air raid shelter was made from corrugated, galvanised sheet steel. Dad fitted it together, dug the deep hole, placed the shelter and covered it with earth and grass sods. It was a cold, damp place but was supposed to be safe during an air raid. It proved itself, for after a night of bombing we emerged to find that a direct hit on the terraced houses, two doors away, had flattened fifteen dwellings.

*

The house was sad. Suddenly mum wasn't there; dad didn't explain, but smiled a lot at us and patted us frequently. Something was wrong. I asked my elder brother, Herbert, but he didn't know. We missed mum.

Dad started giving us money to go to the cinema every day. We went to the Balfour Cinema and saw *Pinocchio*. At first it was a luxury but after watching it for five afternoons, even that paled and mum came into our thoughts.

Auntie Emily lived next door and saw to our meals. If I cried for mum, Herbert would try and cheer me up, but he was as miserable as me.

One day we were called into the house from our play. Two very big men were sitting in the back room. They wore dark suits. One sat me on his knee. Dad stood saying nothing. They asked questions about my dad. Were we getting enough to eat? What time did we go to bed? Dad was smiling at me. They stood, one of them ruffled my hair and they left. Auntie came in. Dad swore. We went out to play again. Mum had left dad.

Mum's absence meant we ran wild. We stayed up as late as we liked, did what we liked, when we liked. We grew increasingly dirty, washing very, very rarely. We got into mischief.

We hated mum for leaving us but missed her terribly and

longed to see her. Her face faded from my mind, I couldn't remember what she looked like.

Dad was drunk every night. Although we were in bed when he got home from the pub we'd hear him crashing about downstairs. In the afternoons he was running a card gambling school. The house was full of dubious characters. He was visiting the coin tossing ring that was hidden in Tinsley Park Woods and losing money. He wasn't shaving and looked a wreck.

One night as we lay asleep, suddenly there was a terrific banging at the bedroom window. We shot bolt upright in bed, frightened out of our wits. Outside, on the lavatory roof, we saw the shape of someone. It was dad, shouting. Herbert went to the window and slid it open. Dad half climbed in and half fell in. Drunk again. He had a silly smile on his face and reeked of beer.

"It's alright son, it's only your dad," he slurred, "I forgot my key. Go back to sleep."

He stumbled round the bed and out onto the landing, then thumped down the stairs in the dark. We heard the kitchen door sneck shut as he went out to the lavatory. Minutes later there was a loud cursing as once more he started to climb onto the lavatory roof. We lay, bursting with laughter as he entered the bedroom for the second time.

"Bleeding door!" was all he said as he left the room.

One day dad called us in from the yard. We were going to the seaside to see mum. The following morning we were on Broughton Lane Railway Station with the posters showing scenes of the coast and country — we were excited. It was a bright morning, not summer because we had our overcoats on. Dad had bought them specially for us, they were orangey coloured, heavy and itchy.

The journey to Bridlington passed without incident, apart from me getting cinders in my eyes through lolling out of the train window.

I remember being inside an enormously big, posh house. There were carpets on the floor and everywhere stood fine polished furniture. Everything was bright. The door opened, and there stood mum. She was wearing a black dress and around her waist was a white apron. We had a holiday with mum and it was as though she had never been out of our lives. We learned she was working in service at the big house. The owners had two daughters who looked after us, took us everywhere and showed us a new and different life. Dad didn't stay with us but returned home. After what seemed months and months, but was only two weeks, we went home to Sheffield, this time with mum. She'd gone back to dad.

From that day, dad altered quite a bit. He still liked to drink, but now in moderation. He started to dress more smartly and decorated the entire house. Mum was happy.

*

The slag heaps held a fascination for us that would at times bubble over, culminating in an expedition. They were situated at the far end of Tinsley Park Woods, or what was left of the scrubby trees and bushes that had been poisoned by the sulphur in the air.

We started out early, taking with us a pop bottle full of water and sandwiches.

"We'll have to be careful with the supplies," Captain Alan informed the explorers. "We could get snowbound tonight and be cut off from everybody in the world."

Captain Enoch frowned. He was ravenous and didn't relish being rationed particularly. He'd missed breakfast in his rush to get to the expedition's starting point.

Rosie handed each of us our personal bundles of bread. Soon we were exchanging potted meat for jam, jam for condensed milk, condensed milk for sugar, sugar for lard, until all the fearless mountaineers had a varied cross section of each other's sandwiches.

Around the base of the towering grey slag heaps were massive flat areas, scarred deep by the countless rains and fires. Bright yellow, sulphur-stained pits and gullies barred our way. The sulphur stank but we didn't notice it after a while, our noses must have become paralysed.

As we approached the great rising heaps the ground grew increasingly warmer. Underneath, fires were raging, consuming the poor quality coal. Here and there the fires had broken surface and sulphurous blue flames and smoke curled into the summer air. We circled these, giving them a wide berth. There were stories of people falling through the surface into the fires of the hollow underground. This was the main reason the area was forbidden to us by our parents, but that added to our sense of daring.

Pretty soon we were hot and sticky, our clothes covered in the 'yellow peril'. Frequent rests and swigs from the bottle helped but the water was always warm and flat and didn't quench our thirst at all, and the courtesy of wiping the top of the bottle soon turned the water a yellowy colour.

Eventually we started to climb, choosing a convenient rain-gouged ravine to make it easier.

"Let's put our climbing equipment on now." Herbert suggested.

Captain Enoch removed the coil of washing line which he had borrowed from his mother's clothes posts, and after a vast amount of struggling, succeeded in roping all the Captains and the two Shirkers together. At last we were ready for the hazardous ascent of the grey-faced Mount Everlast.

"Forward men!" Herbert cried, and took his first step on the unconquered mountain. The rope tightened, he lost his footing and fell onto the loose slag. Captain Enoch giggled.

"It's not funny you know," Herbert glared, rubbing his skinned knee.

Rosie, seeing the blood, rushed forward, anxious to administer first aid. In her haste, she forgot she was tethered to Shirker Margaret.

"Blinking 'eck!" Margaret exclaimed as she shot off her feet and landed heavily on a pile of sulphur-coloured stones.

Captain Enoch giggled again. Margaret's temper flared and she pulled hard on the line. Enoch lost his balance, stumbled, and then joined Herbert and Margaret on the ground, bringing with him Captain Barry, Captain Alan, Captain Brian and me. The expedition was reduced to chaos even before we had vacated base camp.

"I will climb solo," Captain Herbert announced.

"Not a bad idea," Captain Alan agreed.

Not venturing to stand, we all sat and freed ourselves from the life line. Enoch re-coiled the thin rope, slung it over his shoulder, and regretted borrowing it now that its use as an essential piece of equipment had been discarded. At the time he'd judged that the clip around the ear when it was discovered he'd removed it would be worth the risk, but seeing it now hanging redundantly over his shoulder, the enormity of his crime hit him. After all it was Monday, and Monday was the traditional day for all mothers to perpetuate the age old ritual of clean clothes becoming dirty clothes to become clean clothes.

Enoch sighed, gazed across the distant roof tops, and saw the hundreds of full washing lines fluttering in the smoky air, then noted with a shudder one empty backyard.

He sighed again, turned away, and began scrambling ever higher to catch the Captains and the Shirkers who had reached the snow line.

Achieving the top always gave us a sense of freedom. To stand there and survey the distant houses and factories through the hazy-blue atmosphere was magic. On the summit was the twisted pylon of a disused bucket tower used to support the cables that once carried the discarded slag, which we called the 'aeroplane'. At the top of the heap the buckets would tip and shower the rubbish down to add to the enormous pile. Long since, the pylon had assumed a crazy angle. The side of the slag heap towards which it leaned had been eroded away by the rains and wind to form a concave scoop in the dirt. We'd climb the gantry and pull ourselves hand over hand to overhang the scoop far below. Once, I slipped. My hand caught on a rusting girder and I was falling. My fall was broken when I hit the soft shale at an angle and I continued tumbling over and over until, all momentum gone, I came to rest on my stomach, unhurt, but very shaken.

I looked up and far, far above me my brother still hung staring down at me. Regaining the slag, he took giant strides, pushing great avalanches of dirt in front of him as he raced towards me. We laughed and laughed and in a mad race slithered and fell to the bottom of the heap.

On the way home we grabbed handfuls of elderberries from the bushes and ate them together with 'bread and cheese', hawthorn leaves. If we saw a 'piggy nut' plant we'd dig down to its roots and, finding the nodules, rub off the dirt and eat them.

As we approached our houses, we saw to our ablutions, spitting on our hands and plastering it on our hair in an attempt to hide our appearance. It never worked. We always looked like Chinese, with purple lips.

*

Come Fridays, mum would go to Tommy's, the pawnbroker, to fetch dad's suit out for the weekend. That navy-blue suit was in and out of pawn so often it could have found its own way there. In summer, the few winter blankets that had been on the beds were bundled up into brown paper parcels and I would help to cart them to Tommy's where mum pledged them for a few shillings. The pawnbroker's shop door was heavily barred and padlocked. Inside, the counter was shoulder high on mum. Tommy would ummm and arrr, beating mum down in price on what she had taken. He always won — I hated him. Two shillings for my dad's suit, and my dad didn't half look smart in it on Saturday nights with his white silk muffler and his best flat hat. Out it came on Friday afternoon and in it went on Monday morning, week in, week out. If articles were not redeemed after a certain length of time, Tommy could legally claim them to sell in the shop. His window was full of the most unlikely objects, all pledged for a pittance and sold at a colossal profit. Talk about feeding on poverty, that man was an expert. Sometimes there was panic on Friday afternoons if mum couldn't find the pawn ticket, but it always turned up after much searching behind the ornaments on the cornice or under the pot dogs on the sideboard. Dad once pawned his garden spade, when he was off work sick.

*

Summers were hot and dry, the sun shone down every day, or so it seemed. It was warm and daylight until well after ten o'clock. People sat on their doorsteps and talked quietly into the night. It was too hot to go indoors and sleep in the hothouse bedrooms that had baked under the slates all day. There was a saying that if you weren't in bed by twelve o'clock the bugs and fleas would come and fetch you.

Next door to our house lived Mrs Brigham. Mrs Brigham thought she was posher and cleaner than us but the gang knew she kept chickens and rabbits in her front room. There was always a net curtain up to the window but if you pressed your face close you could see through the holes and there they were, pecking and strutting about on the droppings-covered floor. We'd stand howling like dogs and the chickens would go berserk inside. She chased us with her yard brush down the road if she heard us. We were never caught because her mind was constantly befuddled with gin which she secretly swigged throughout the day.

The gang stood by the gas-lamp and watched with interest as Mr Brigham knelt on all fours outside his house and had a conversation with his coal cellar grate.

"What's he doing?" Barry asked.

"Talking to the pavement," Rosie answered.

We giggled. Mr Brigham turned and glared at us. We pretended to be occupied with other things.

He bent his head closer to the grate and began talking once again. Slowly the gang sidled across the road and sat on the kerb edge, the better to watch and listen.

"Well it was a bloody daft thing to do," he hissed at the cast iron cover, "You know I've no key for that lock."

Rosie bent close to us and whispered, "He's gone loony or he's drunk. Talking to a grate!" We giggled again. Mr Brigham spun on us. "Look, sod off you little buggers!"

We sat our ground. Suddenly and faintly we heard the cellar grate answer him.

"I'm sorry, love, I forgot. What shall we do?"

Mr Brigham pushed his flat cap to the back of his head, scratched his ear, thought for a moment, then said, "Look, woman, there's a screw driver in me cobbling box. Use that on the screws."

There was a pause as Mrs Brigham climbed to their kitchen, found the cobbling box, and retrieved the screw driver. Mr Brigham stood, and with a snarling glance at the gang, disappeared down the entry. His voice echoed back to the street. "Are you there woman? Have you found it?" Then louder, "Have you found it yet?"

We sat watching the free show and heard the faint voice of Mrs Brigham issue from the grate.

"Jack...Jack...are you there love? Jack?"

Rosie crossed to the entry. "Mr Brigham! Mrs Brigham is shouting up the cellar grate!"

He turned, glared, and with a face like thunder, returned to the cellar grate. On all fours once more he shouted, "What you doing down there again. Did you find the screw driver?"

"Yes love."

"Well, why aren't you at the gate, you silly sod?"

"Which way does the screw driver work?" she asked.

"Both ways, you barmpot — women, I don't know — now go and undo the hasp screws or we'll be here all night."

Mrs Lindley appeared at the top of her entry. She was carrying a bucket and coal shovel. She glanced with scant interest at Mr Brigham, walked towards us, stepped into the road and scooped up the by-products of the rag-and-bone man's horse to further nourish her rhubarb.

In a less fraught situation Mr Brigham would have protested the ownership of the manure, it being outside his house and therefore under the protection of squatter's rights, but on this occasion he let the matter slide and Mrs Lindley turned to retrace her shuffling steps back to her garden, with a smirk on her face.

"Have you gone woman?" he called at the cellar lid. Silence. He stood once more and, reaching the bottom of the entry, faced the locked gate. "Right woman," his voice reverberated, "unscrew them four screws on the hasp side."

We all shuffled along the kerb until the entry acted as a real bioscope with the gang craning their necks to see all the action. "Have you done it yet, woman?" he hissed through the wooden door.

"Nearly love, just one to go."

"I don't know! Why you locked the thing in the first place is beyond me, you know I haven't got a key for it."

"But they keep pinching the bin," Mrs Brigham answered.

"Who do?"

"I don't know, love, that's why I locked it, to stop them pinching the bin."

"Who'd want our rubbish?" Mr Brigham snapped.

"I don't know. Somebody does though. One minute I was putting the hot ashes from the fire in it, the next it was gone."

Suddenly the gate swung open and Mrs Brigham stood beaming a smile at her husband, "There we are love."

He pushed past her and snarled, "And tha can wipe that silly grin off thee face! What's for tea?"

Mrs Brigham didn't answer, but followed her husband meekly into the house and wondered how she was going to explain her lapse of memory regarding his uncooked meal.

Now that the free show was over the gang wandered from the road and, crossing the bombed site, made for our favourite grassy hollow, behind the vicarage, adjacent to the allotments where we threw ourselves down and stretched out on the soft grass to gaze into the sky.

"Me mam says life's a bowl of cherries," Rosie announced.

"That's stupid", Enoch said, "What's it mean, life's a bowl of cherries?"

"Don't know, but me mam says it is."

"My dad says there's no rest for the wicked," Barry said.

"What's that mean?" Enoch asked. "That's another burk of a saying."

"Never look a gift horse in the mouth," Herbert said. "Our mam is always saying that, in't she, Walt?"

Enoch was beginning to have doubts regarding all our parents' sanity. The only phrases Enoch's mother used were "Go outside and play!" or "Get out from under me feet!" These he understood. They were plain statements, orders to be obeyed. But to have parents talking about fruit, horses and wicked people would, he was sure, confuse his simple, no-nonsense, life-style. He imagined his dad putting his fatherly arm around his shoulders and saying, "You know son, life is just a bowl of cherries."

"Yes dad, I know it is, but don't let that gift horse's mouth near them or he will scoff the lot."

"Whenever my Uncle Ted comes to our house he always asks me how many beans make five," Herbert said. "Every time he comes. He thinks it's a great joke. Me mam always laughs and I always laugh as well and say I don't know."

"Why?" Alan asked.

"'Cos if I say I don't know, he tells me and gives me a penny. I'm not daft."

The gang realised Herbert was sitting on a gold mine and were envious. We lapsed into silence and chewed on our individual stalks of grass. Eventually Barry broke the silence.

"Wonder who's pinched her bin?" he asked. "Whose bin?" Rosie questioned.

"Mrs Brigham's bin," Barry replied. "Who'd want a bin full of rubbish?"

Now here was a mystery if ever there was one. One by one we sat up and applied our minds to the puzzle. Clothes props, garden tools, even washing from clothes lines, these were fair game for neighbourhood burglars, but dustbins? Who'd want to thieve a dustbin? And not only a dustbin, but a dustbin full of hot ashes and tea leaves. This was indeed the Marie Celeste enigma of Coleford Road.

"Perhaps it wasn't pinched," said Margaret. "Perhaps she lost it. Me mother's always misplacing things."

"Lost it?" Herbert said incredulously, "Lost it? How can

you lose a dustbin? You burk."

Margaret dropped her head and sulked. "I only said perhaps," she mumbled.

"Perhaps somebody collects them," Brian said, "You know, for a hobby, like we collect stamps and things."

Another chorus of jeers.

"Perhaps the burglar's bin is full and he wants another." Alan said brightly.

Now this seemed more likely. After all the bin collections could be rather erratic sometimes, especially at holiday periods.

"Me mam just piles our rubbish at the side if it's full," Enoch sniffed.

"Yes I know that," Herbert said. "But there's some around here who worship their bins. Look at Mr Cockington, every time they empty his bin he washes it inside and out and he polishes the handles. It took him three days to paint his house number on it once. And he wraps every piece of rubbish up individually. Oh yes, he loves his bin alright. There's all hell on if he doesn't get his proper bin back at collection days."

"Well, if I was Mr Cockington I wouldn't pinch Mrs Brigham's bin. It would take him a year to get it clean," Rosie said.

There was no escaping this logic. Some time later we watched as Mr Frieze the vicar, walked slowly up the cart track towards his vicarage. He drew level, spotted us in the hollow, crossed, and stood in front of us.

"Good afternoon children, are you being good?"

"Yes, Mr Frieze," we all answered.

"Good, good." he replied, "Don't forget to come to church on Sunday will you?"

"No, Mr Frieze."

"Good, Good."

"Somebody's pinched Mrs Brigham's bin, Mr Frieze." Rosie blurted out.

"Dear, dear. That is naughty of them," he exclaimed, "Still I suppose it will turn up. God moves in mysterious ways. Goodbye children." He turned and swished away.

"He does it as well," Enoch said.

"Does what?" I asked.

"Says things that don't make sense. God moves in mysterious ways. God hasn't pinched the bin has he? Why bring him into it?"

"'Cos he's a holy man," Rosie defended. "He has to keep saying things with God in them, stands to reason. He can't say, 'Dear, dear, that's naughty. I hope they catch the buggers.' He has to say good things all the time."

Far away we heard the sound of the rag-and-bone man's call. "Donkey stone for old rags-o!" It drew nearer, then suddenly the calling stopped. Gradually we heard the sound of galloping hooves and the urgent call of "Wooew, you silly sod!" It grew louder.

We stood to see what the commotion was. Suddenly around the bend in the track the horse and cart appeared. It was bounding along at a furious pace with the neckerchiefed rag man clinging on for dear life. From the back of the cart great billows of smoke and flames belched into the air.

His entire day's collection was on fire, and the horse was out of control, trying to flee the flames. The faster it ran, the more the fire was fanned. The rag man cursed and roared at the animal. We watched in amazement as they drew level then thundered past, to disappear round the sharp bend that led to the stable. The inferno caught a rock in the cart track. It tilted crazily on one wheel. The load slipped. There was a bang and a clatter and we watched with wide eyes as Mrs Brigham's bin slid from under the burning rags and fell into the hedge, spilling smouldering ashes into the bushes. We stood rooted to the spot and stared after the disappearing rag cart.

After the noise and screaming suddenly everything was strangely quiet.

"Did you see that?" Enoch whispered. "Mrs Brigham's bin!"

So it was the rag man who had done the dirty deed.

"Hey!" Alan shouted, "Let's get it, there's bound to be a reward for finding it." The gang ran to where the smouldering bin lay on its side in the grass.

"We'll have to get the rest of the ashes out and let it cool off first," Herbert said, and using sticks from the hedge they removed the rest of the contents.

It cooled quickly in the evening air and with Barry and Enoch holding a handle each, the procession set off towards Mrs Brigham's house and the anticipated reward.

We stood outside the kitchen door of Mrs Brigham's. Enoch reached and knocked loudly. From inside came the muffled sound of a chair being scraped back. Footsteps approached, and the door was flung wide. There before us stood Mr Brigham with the evening paper in one hand, a mug of tea in the other, and his braces dangling around his knees.

"What do you want?" he growled.

"We've brought yer bin back," Alan said proudly.

The gang moved to one side to reveal the bin.

"Is there a reward, Mr Brigham?" Enoch asked eagerly.

Mr Brigham looked first at the bin then at the members of the gang. Slowly his face turned purple, his hands clenched until the knuckles showed white, "A reward? A reward? First you pinch the bin then you bring it back and expect a reward?"

Enoch began to protest our innocence but it fell on deaf ears. Mr Brigham had already found us guilty. There was no appeal.

"I'll give you a bloody reward alright!" He made to undo his thick leather belt. The action was familiar to us all. With one accord we turned, and without a glance back, we fled the yard and didn't stop running until we reached our den on the bomb site.

"That wasn't fair," Brian said breathlessly, "He thinks we pinched his rotten bin."

After some ten minutes of destroying Mr and Mrs Brigham's character, we calmed down and sat in silence.

Quietly Rosie said, "I wonder what the rag and bone man wanted the bin for anyway?"

Enoch thought for a moment, visualised the stables interior, spotted two similar bins, smiled as realisation dawned, and said, "To keep the horse's drinking water in of course!"

He stood preening himself for solving the great bin mystery.

*

The Darnall Bug Hut was just that, crawling. But every Saturday afternoon we queued outside, clutching our pennies, eager to get in. When the doors were opened, the term 'penny rush' became a reality. We'd mob through the door and, handing our pennies over, push past the ragged velvet curtain into the foetid atmosphere of the tiny cinema.

The dirty, old attendant pushed us along the forms, squeezing as many of us as he could onto the hard, splintery benches. Within a few short minutes the place was a hot house of shouting, stamping, crying hooligans. The youngest and weakest were pushed to the front forms and had to endure the neck-breaking ordeal of watching the pictures with their heads tilted back at right angles to their bodies.

The lights went out unceremoniously and a great roar would go up as the first picture flickered onto the sagging, off-white screen. The attendant constantly passed amongst us, a clip here, a cuff there, and curses everywhere, as he tried to maintain order whilst *Johnny Mac Brown* wrestled with the baddie on the screen and we wrestled with the nearest neighbour on the form, in our mind's eye helping Johnny.

As the show progressed, the attendant passed down the aisle with a great brass and copper sprayer, directing the scented disinfectant spray into the air to descend onto our close-cropped heads in an effort to keep the bugs quiet.

Zorro slashed his way across the Mexican landscape, marking everything and everybody in his path with a 'Z'. Roy Rogers fought off twenty bad men, his hat never once falling from his head, and then sang a sloppy song to some girl; we'd boo at that and old 'Spray-can Sam' beat a few more tortured young bodies into quiet submission. *The Three Stooges*, Curly, Larry and Mo, creased us up with laughter at their own brand of mayhem. At the interval, the ice-cream woman disappeared at the foot of the aisle under hundreds of sweaty, shouting kids while 'Spray-can Sam' used the mob to practise his deadly rabbit punch on small necks.

Lights out and into the second half; the smell of urine coming from youngsters too preoccupied by the films to fight their way to the one toilet. The place was like an oven and 'Spray-can Sam's' one concession to keeping us from suffocating was to open the fire door at the side and let the air billow in past the dirty, red velvet curtains. The kids near the door could hardly see the picture flickering on the screen as the daylight glare killed the reflection. They started to chant, "Give us us money back!" and were immediately quelled as Sam swung into action.

For the umpteenth time, the screen went blank as the film snapped in the projector. Pitch black pandemonium! Kids yelled and booed! Sam slashed out at frail bodies in the dark, enjoying the anonymous thrill; soft skin was bruised and broken. Sam was *Zorro*!

And so it went on until the final film died on the screen. As the lights went up, the first bar of the National Anthem rang out; the second bar would play to a completely empty cinema, cleared in five seconds flat, leaving 'Sam' and the manager alone in ankle-deep filth.

Out in the mid-afternoon glare, our heads burst with pain from the bright sun. Buttoning navy-blue raincoats around our necks to form a cape, we *Zorroed* our way home to bread and jam for tea.

*

Saturday night; Dad dressed up and clean. Mum in her long black coat with its real fur collar. Second hand, imitation pearl earrings and curling-tonged hair completed her best outfit. They were going to the pub.

We stood in our blue and white striped pyjamas after our bath. Saturday night was always bath and nit night. Dad fetched the large tin bath from its nail outside in the yard and, placing it in front of the fire, mum half filled it with hot water from the cast iron kettle which rattled on the fire. Pans also boiled, in fact anything that held water and could stand the fire was pressed into service.

When sufficient water steamed in the bath, mum tested it with her elbow, pronounced it alright, and my brother and I climbed in. The side closest to the fire grew red hot, keeping the water warm. As mum scrubbed away at us I'd pass the time scraping the side of the bath of its thick layer of dried soap accumulated over many baths.

Afterwards, squeaky clean and dry, we had to submit to the nit comb. In turn we'd kneel in front of mum and lower our heads onto her knees. She'd comb every strand of our hair with the needle sharp teeth of the special comb, looking for nits and dicks. If the comb dug in we'd yell out and jump, only to have our heads pressed firmly between mum's knees, clamped shut to prevent further escapes. This over, our vinegar-rinsed hair was combed neatly.

Mum always said the same thing; "Now that didn't hurt much did it?" But it did.

Eventually, off they'd go, telling us to be good. On these occasions our cousin, Margaret, baby sat us. Pretty soon Rosie Bacon turned up at the house and came in. We played games, doctors and nurses being favourite with the girls. The surgery was under a white sheet over an armchair. Doctor Margaret and Doctor Rosie took it in turns to examine our nether regions. I wasn't keen and couldn't see any fun in it at nine years old, but it seemed to provide endless fascination to the older girls.

Tiring of that we wandered out into the yard and up the entry onto the street, playing in our pyjamas until the sun set. Spotting mum and dad turning the corner, we scuttled back into the house and up to bed. We lay with eyes tight shut and felt mum bend across us, kiss us and whisper, "Good night, God bless."

Some Saturday nights we were left on our own. I didn't like that. Herbert switched on the wireless and listened to *The Man In Black* and *Saturday Night Theatre*. Some of the plays scared me silly and I curled up in a chair with my hands over my ears trying to block out the screams and groans coming from the radio. At other times I absent-mindedly played with the fire using the brush in the hearth to brush the red hot bars until the bristles smouldered and caught fire. Quickly extinguishing it, I would start the whole fascinating business again. When mum and dad arrived home it was always the same;

"Have you been burning the brush again, Walter?"

"No mam."

She'd pick it up out of the hearth look at its burnt black stubble, sniff the air and turning say, "Mr Nobody I suppose."

*

Sunday: up bright and early for church. We met in the vestry to change into cassock and surplice for Morning Service. Then, like little angels, we followed the cross down the aisle to the choir stalls to sing our way through the service, with pauses for psalms and prayers.

We were a cherub-voiced lot, if cherubs in heaven sang with thick Yorkshire accents which wandered up and down scales and changed keys at the slightest whim. Belonging to the choir was the one concession we made to human conformity, and even this had to be enforced by frequent threats from mothers. Our rendition of *Abide With Me* would have reduced any ship's captain to despair even in the midst of a sinking, but the hymn that we excelled at, and the one that was guaranteed to make even the church's cracked bell seem melodic, was our favourite *Fight The Good Fight*. When Enoch was seized by religious fervour he let rip and punctuated the words with wild arm gestures.

Indeed, on not a few occasions he had to be restrained by adult members of the choir who feared for the safety of his innocent mind and the rickety choir stalls.

Despite frequent requests from the female members of the congregation, Mr Frieze, the vicar, refused to refurbish the choir with new blood, saying, "They are all God's creatures and, anyway, I enjoy their harmonising."

Mr Frieze needless to say, had poor hearing and was also tone deaf. Mrs Padley, the organist, was also a strong supporter of the religious singers. She had good reason to be thankful for their discordant renditions, which covered many a missed note caused by her arthritic fingers. All in all, God must have dreaded Sunday mornings, and wished for a lie in, when St Alban's offerings drifted heavenwards.

Still, as Rosie always said when criticism was levelled at us, "If we were brilliant singers, we'd all be singing in a cathedral, not in a pokey church in the middle of the steelworks." There was no answer to this.

"You carried it last week, it's not fair! It's my turn this week," Margaret argued, as she struggled to free the swaying brass cross from Enoch's grasp. "You always carry it, Enoch Thompson, let somebody else have a turn!"

"I always carry it because I'm the best cross carrier this church has got. It teks practise, does cross carrying." Enoch and Margaret continued to struggle. "Mr Frieze says I've got religious hair and I know just how fast to walk down the aisle with it. You'd be legging everybody up at each step."

"No, I wouldn't," Margaret snapped back, "If I'd had as many turns at cross carrying as you, I'd be just as good; so let go of it and let me carry it today."

"Not likely," Enoch replied, "If you made a mess of it, God would be dead mad. Don't forget it's His day, today, Sunday, He'd be watching every step you made. I'm not risking His broth from heaven."

With a quick twist of his wrist, he wrenched the carved staff free of Margaret's hands and hugged it to his chest.

Margaret stood fighting back the tears of frustration as she glared at him with hate-filled eyes. "You're dead mardy, Enoch Thompson. And you're unholy!" She spat the words out.

"I'm holier than you anyway," Enoch replied, "I'm a cross carrier, first class! Not like you, you couldn't even carry a... a... feather without dropping it."

Margaret stuck her tongue out as far as she could, then crossed the dusty vestry to join Rosie who was struggling to put on her off-white surplice.

"Take no notice of him, Margaret," Rosie said, "You can come and help me fill the font." The two girls left the vestry and returned some minutes later carrying a polished brass jug.

"There's no Holy water," Rosie announced, and turned the jug upside down to prove the point, "Mr Frieze must have forgotten to get some."

"He gets it out of the tap. It's only tap water," Brian said, as he fastened the buttons of his cassock.

"Don't be daft," Rosie exclaimed, "Tap water indeed! It's special water he uses for christenings, it's church water. It's special, is that."

"What's special about it?" Alan asked, as he spat on the collection plate and began polishing it. "It all comes from the same dam."

"Yes it might come from the same dam as all the other water, but," Rosie paused, "but Mr Frieze turns it holy before he uses it."

"Well, I wouldn't worry," Enoch said, "He'll be in soon, then you can tell him. Shouldn't tek him long to holify a bucketful for you."

From the far end of the church the flat tone of the solitary bell began to call the faithful to worship as Mr Pringle, the lapsed Jewish pork butcher, pulled on the much knotted rope. In the far corner of the vestry Mr Lindley began practising his scales, without once removing the half-smoked cigarette from between his lips. As he hit the upper register of his very limited range, he began to cough profusely. Mr Johnson, the full-time insurance man, part-time scout master, and quarter-time tally man, thumped Mr Lindley's back, in an effort to relieve the coughing fit.

"With a bit of luck," Barry whispered, "there'll be a funeral soon." He inclined his head towards Mr Lindley.

Alan nodded and winked in agreement. Funerals and weddings were high on the choir's list of favourite functions, bringing tips from the mourners at each event.

The door to the vestry opened, and Mr Frieze strode into the midst of the choir.

"Good morning, everyone," he said, with practised cheerfulness.

The choir mumbled, "Good morning," and resumed their struggle with the holy clothes.

"Mr Frieze," Rosie piped up. "Mr Frieze, we've no holy water for the font."

"Haven't we, young Rosie?" he replied, "Well you'd best fill it up from the tap in the kitchen sink."

Rosie's jaw dropped open. Brian looked across at her and smirked knowingly.

"Right, everyone," Mr Frieze addressed the choir, "This week's hymns will be the usual first four, but to finish with I thought we'd have hymn number, four five three for a change."

"Oh no," Mr Lindley thought. "Not *Nearer to God am I* I hate that one." He removed the tab end that was now scorching his lips and had another quiet coughing fit.

"During the second verse...," Mr Frieze paused and asked, "Who's on the collection plate?"

Alan held the brass dish above his head.

"Ah, young Alan, is it? Well, as I was saying, during the second verse, Alan, start passing the plate along the rows. Not so fast this week, take your time. We missed a ten shilling note from Mrs Chippinghouse last week. We can't have that, can we?" He smiled pointedly at Alan. Alan shook his head. "Oh and before I forget, keep your eyes peeled. Last week there were more buttons and washers than ever before."

Alan nodded his head.

"My sermon this week will be entitled, 'Poverty is better than being rich, if you can do without money'." The choir looked at him mystified, and wondered if Mr Frieze was really in tune with reality. "It will last exactly twelve minutes and during that time I would be grateful if certain members of this choir didn't have a fit of the giggles when Mrs Padley dozes off. Her snoring is a condition brought on by her very bad chest. Mrs Padley's chest is no laughing matter."

"You can say that again," Mr Johnson said under his breath. Mr Lindley smirked.

"Right then. I think that is all. Shall we all line up and proceed down the aisle to do God's work and give the Devil one hell of a time?"

Enoch took his place behind the vicar and the rest formed up in twos behind him. Mr Frieze opened the vestry door and stood waiting for the organ music to whimper through the church. Mrs Padley glanced through her rear view mirror, caught sight of the holy man, freed the handbrake, eased the clutch in, and proceeded erratically down the first verse of the opening hymn.

From the corner of his mouth Mr Frieze muttered, "Left foot first everybody, go!" and the procession was on its way. Margaret's left foot for some reason was on the right side of her body and so, at every step Alan's heel was mutilated, until he changed his step, and began mutilating Brian's. Soon everybody in Margaret's line fell in step to avoid the pain. But now another problem became evident; at each step the two lines opened and closed resulting in shoulders crashing into each other.

Margaret whispered across to Rosie, "Half this lot ought to learn to walk religiously before they join a choir, it looks a right mess."

Rosie nodded in agreement.

"Look at that cross, it's swaying all over the place. I telled you he was a rubbish cross carrier."

Again Rosie nodded.

Enoch was in dire straits. The safety pin holding his trousers up had broken, and as well as receiving severe wounds at each step, he could feel his trousers beginning to desert him inch by inch.

The procession reached the choir stalls and the lines peeled away to their allotted places. But Enoch's ordeal was not over. Being the bearer, he continued behind Mr Frieze towards the steps of the altar to place the cross in its holder. He could feel all eyes watching his every step. Summoning up a last effort, he slotted the staff into the tube with as much religious dignity as his situation would allow, then turned and with his knees akimbo, waddled ape-like to his seat. With a sigh he sat down with his trousers around his ankles.

"Look at him larking about, it's disgusting," Margaret said, "He's not fit to carry a cross, I don't care what anybody says."

Rosie didn't answer. She was too busy dreaming of Enoch's white thighs.

The service staggered and stumbled to its end. Mr Frieze's sermon was as well received as the smallpox. The collection plate yielded the sum of five shillings and sixpence, plus eight buttons, four washers, and an anonymous note accusing Mr Frieze of being a spy. Alan had beaten Barry at noughts and crosses by fifty games to one. Mr Lindley had managed a crafty smoke behind the thick stone pillar which supported a roof truss. Enoch had successfully carried out emergency repairs to his tattered trousers, and Margaret and Rosie had delighted in embarrassing a pimply youth who sat three rows back and blushed each time he felt their eyes on him. All in all it had been another average Sunday morning at St Alban's and now the gang longed for the freedom of the sunlit outdoors.

Back in the vestry, we quickly removed our hymn singing outfits and with a hundred 'Taras' we all ran from the vestry and out into the fresh air.

Bounding across the broken bricks and rubble, we were soon on no man's land and back amongst familiar surroundings. Herbert reached our hollow first and jumped down into the circular clearing, shouting breathlessly, "I've won! I'm first!"

We all arrived and sat heavily down on our individual house bricks to recover our breath.

"Wonder what's for dinner?" Enoch said.

"We're having corned beef hash," Barry replied.

"We're having rabbit and onion gravy," I added.

"We're having 'Johnny Curnudgeits'," Rosie said.

"Wonder what God has for his dinner?" Enoch asked.

"Anything he wants," Rosie answered. "He'll just conjure up whatever he fancies."

"Must be great being God," Enoch said wistfully.

"Shouldn't think so," Margaret said, "I wouldn't fancy listening to Mrs Padley's playing, and Mr Frieze's daft sermons straight after breakfast, or..." Margaret looked pointedly at Enoch, "watching a burk trying to carry a cross properly. It's enough to put anyone off their food, is that."

Enoch's blood boiled. His fists clenched automatically, and he did an unforgivable thing. He hit a fellow Christian on God's special day.

*

Rosie Bacon's biology classes were always well attended by our gang. It wasn't that we purposely made an effort to be there, it was more like opportunism on the part of Rosie. Usually we'd be sat on the house bricks, in a circle, in our favourite hollow on the bomb site, discussing the war and what we'd do to any caught Germans.

Rosie would pipe up, "I know where babies come from." If that didn't stop us talking she'd continue in a louder voice, "I said, I know where babies come from."

Eventually someone would take the bait and answer, "So what, so do I."

Rosie had caught her fish.

"No you don't," she menaced.

"I do."

"Where from then, clever dick?"

"I'm not telling you, and same to you with knobs on."

"He don't know," Rosie would taunt, looking at us for approval.

We, not wishing to appear ignorant, smiled along with Rosie and sneered at her victim.

"Alright then, Miss Clever Clogs, tell us."

"I will," Rosie answered triumphantly, now that she'd made her opening and had our attention. And so we'd be treated to naughty information.

"You'll have to come closer, I'm not going to shout."

We edged our house bricks into a tight circle around Rosie then she began.

"This is gospel truth, so don't ever tell anybody, alright?"

Vigorous nods of heads and wide eyes all round as Rosie revelled in the undivided attention.

"Well," she continued, "and I mean it about not telling anybody, alright?"

"Yes."

"Well, and this is true, honest... and don't you tell your Margaret, Barry."

"I won't... she'll know already anyway."

"She doesn't cos I haven't telled her."

"No, but she's got a book from t'Church."

"Church doesn't know. All they know about is where God comes from."

"Where's God come from?" one of the Thompson lads asked.

"I don't know. I said Church knows that. Heaven I suppose."

"He doesn't, my mam says he's all around us and this isn't heaven is it? Heaven's up there," piped in our Herbert.

"If heaven's up there, and God's in it, how come he doesn't fall out onto us?" asked our Barry.

"He has a big chair and he sits in it all day listening to prayers and people asking for things. That's why he doesn't fall on us, clever clogs." Herbert threw back his answer with false assurance.

"Did he mek chair his self or did angels help him?"

"I don't know. God doesn't tell you everything you know, he leaves you to find out things from other people."

Rosie jumped in, "Yes, like me, and where babies come from." She beamed. We turned back to her not understanding. "You know I said I'd tell you where babies come from," she answered our quizzical looks.

"Oh yeah, go on then."

"Right I will. Well, it's like this." We were now back on Rosie's favourite subject. "No telling, alright? Cross your heart and hope to die?" We crossed our hearts.

Our Barry didn't.

"Barry didn't cross his heart," Rosie accused.

"Cross your heart, Barry," we urged.

"I crossed it when you weren't looking just now."

"You didn't."

"I did."

"You didn't."

"Oh, shurrup and tell us."

"Well," said Rosie, her voice dropping again, "It's like this. Babies, and don't tell anybody, babies come out of your mam's belly button."

She stood triumphant, smiling and nodding at us. We sat staring at her, digesting this unexpected information. Someone giggled. Rosie spun round to face him. It was one of the Thompsons.

"It's true I tell you, they do." Rosie was losing ground and she sensed it. "They come out of your mam's belly button. You did, I did, we all did. It's true."

The next question had to come, it was the jackpot question. Barry asked it.

"How they get in there then, clever clogs?"

Rosie stood; you could practically see her brain working overtime. "Er...well...er...it's like this. Your mam goes to the doctor's and tells him she wants a baby. He says alright and gets a big needle and sticks it in your mam's belly and puts you in, very small."

"How small?"

"Smaller than a rabbit."

"Smaller than a bed bug?"

"No, not that small," retorted Rosie.

"Bigger than a bed bug then?"

"Yes, of course."

"Must be a big needle," Herbert muttered.

Rosie spun on him; "Course it's a big needle."

"Bet it hurts."

"Course it hurts, but that's because your mam loves and wants you." We couldn't argue that.

"How do you come out then?". Another question for Doctor Rosie. She didn't falter this time, but launched into a detailed explanation of our births.

"When you've had enough food and drink and you want to come out and see your mam and dad, what you do is cry right loud. Your mam hears you and goes to the doctor's to tell him you're crying inside her. He has a listen and, if it's true, he says, 'You're going to have a baby, go home and rest a lot.' Then your mam goes home and tells your dad she's going to have a baby . They hold hands and kiss a lot!" Rosie had us in her spell, and she continued. "After some time your mam gets fat with eating, and has to wear big frocks and hold her back a lot. She buys balls of wool and knits you clothes to keep her busy."

"How's she know us size?" Ever sceptical Barry asked.

"Doctor tells her."

That seemed reasonable. Rosie continued; "When you're ready to be born, when your mam's knitted enough clothes for you, your dad sends for old lass Biggins and she goes upstairs with your mam to wash all the knitted things your mam's made. She makes your dad take up a lot of hot water when she's washing while your mam lies on the bed and watches her. After a bit you're born and cry for some milk and then you sleep with your mother until you can walk. And that's where babies come from, but don't tell anybody."

We swore an oath of silence and then over the coming weeks told everybody.

My Grandma Glasby lived in a spotless, cosy, small terraced house. She was all that a grandmother should be — an elfish round face which was always smiling; chubby, cuddly arms; a comfortable body; and a capacity for hard work that I now look back on with awe. She was tiny but her presence always commanded attention. She didn't waste words so when she spoke my mother or her brother and sisters listened. My dad rebelled against her and they didn't get on. She looked down on his drinking and his boozing partners.

In winter I sometimes went straight from infants school to Grandma's. At half past three it was just going dark and at Gran's she never put the light on so pretty soon the room was only lit by the red glow from the fire grate. I sat on the pegged rug in front of the fire, the heat making me drowsy. Gran toasted bread up to the bars of the grate and we ate hot toast with margarine on it. Afterwards I fell asleep on the rug in front of the blaze, feeling the warmth drive out the cold. All the while it grew darker outside until the gas lamps in the road were lit and the yellowy-green glow would enter and shine on the polished furniture. Gran sat quietly in her rocking chair occasionally poking the fire to clear the ashes. Grandma's was great. She never pestered us with questions but would listen with a smile on her lips to any exciting news we had.

My Grandma's toilet was a sight to behold – a double seater! She scrubbed that double-holed seat until the wood was glass smooth and snow white. It was whitewashed every month. You could always tell when the month was nearly up as the daddy long legs and the spiders' webs grew more and more numerous. She donkey stoned the step outside the door every day no matter the weather. In winter she placed a night light candle in a saucer of water next to the cistern to prevent it freezing during the night. The light also served as a beacon guiding anyone to the toilet as the rays of light glimmered through the cracks in the door. Behind the door, on a nail, hung little neat squares of newspaper, affording a read as well as the obvious use. Having no lock on the door it was always wise to sing or whistle whilst using the facilities. I learned to whistle in there.

Pegging a rug was an art I watched mum and grandma do on countless occasions. They'd usually start in October, to have it ready for Christmas. Dad would obtain two potato sacks from the greengrocers and mum washed them in the copper. When dry, they were cut open and then sewn together with string to make a large square. That was the easy part. For weeks before mum would have been busy at night cutting up old coats, trousers, dresses – anything that could be used and was colourful. The cloth was then cut further into one inch by two inch pieces and sorted into various bags until she'd probably have six or seven different colours. A pattern was drawn on the sacking, the only limiting factor being mum's imagination.

Then the real work would start. For nights on end, week in, week out, she sat by the fire, the sacking over her knees, surrounded by the bags of clippings, pegging away. Using a split, rounded clothes peg, she'd force a strip through the hessian then back again. Row after row, colour after colour, the sacking getting harder to work as the woven strands tightened. Some nights her hands were raw, what with scrubbing floors, washing clothes and pots and pans and finally insulting them with serge cloth, hessian and clothes pegs. When finished the rug looked great for perhaps a month, then gradually the ashes from the fire, the dirt from muddy clogs and spilled food corrupted it into a shabby lump of cloth clippings. A pegged rug couldn't be washed or swept. It's only chance of a clean would come when thrown over the clothes line in the yard and all hell was knocked out of it by dad wielding the flat side of his garden shovel, raising great grey clouds of dust and loose clippings. The sparrows liked the clippings and used them to line their nests up under the gutter.

*

The girls were always putting on concerts. They'd let it be known some time in advance that it was a penny to go in. If interest was lacking, the penny became a halfpenny. The truth was they'd have paid the audience to watch them, so in love with their own image were they. The stage was behind an old sheet thrown across the washing line in the backyard. We boys thought it all a bit of a giggle.
"If you laugh, you're not coming."
"We won't laugh, honest, Rosie."
"If you do Margaret'll thump you, won't you Margaret?"
Margaret nodded between picking her nose.
"What you going to do as an act Rosie?" Barry asked.
"I juggle."
"What with, a ton of loose soot?" one of the Thompson lads muttered under his breath.
"I heard that! You're not coming now."
Margaret struck out, her finger leaving her left nostril with the speed of lightning and together with the rest of her hand, she flattened Brian Thompson. Alan Thompson rallied to his brother's cause and he kicked Margaret. Rosie's nails scraped Alan's arm and Enoch Thompson caught Rosie a punch squarely in her stomach. That was the trouble with fighting a Thompson, you had to take them all on at the same time.
Peace was restored by a shout from Auntie Em's kitchen window; "I'll mek third man if you don't stop fighting out there."

Things calmed down.

"What's Margaret going to do at concert?"

"She," announced Rosie grandly, "she sings, don't you?"

Margaret nodded as she continued to wrestle with her nose.

"What's she sing then?" Herbert asked.

"Oh you know, songs and things, like on the wireless."

"We haven't got a wireless any more," said one of the Thompson's. "This man took it back. For repairing, my mam said."

"I bet you didn't pay weekly on it, that's why," sneered Rosie.

Once again, fists flew.

"I'll mek third man I said!"

Peace was restored.

"Well, if there's only you two, I'm not coming, it'll be a rubbish show," Barry said, and we agreed.

"No wait, there's others, and we do other things, don't we Margaret?"

Margaret nodded, and winced, forgetting where her finger was.

"I also tap dance a bit and I also tight rope walk a bit." Rosie announced hurriedly to keep our attention. We brightened.

"Tight rope walk? Do you?"

"Well, yes, a bit."

"How big a bit?"

"I'm quite good at it. My dad taught me. He learned it when he was in the army." Rosie had recaptured her audience and was relieved.

"We'll come then, if you tight rope walk for us."

"I will, I will, and if I can't do it because I'm poorly or something, Margaret will, won't you?" Rosie menaced.

Margaret removed her finger and said, "Yeah."

Rosie's surprise was ill concealed and she stared disbelievingly at Margaret who was once again turning her nose inside out. We'd caught Rosie and she knew it but she continued bravely on.

"It's a penny to come in you know?"

"I live here," both Herbert and I chorused. "It's our yard."

"It's mine an' all," said Barry. "I live in this yard an' all."

We nodded vigorously. Rosie spoke. "Well, alright then, you three can come for nowt."

"What about us then?" the Thompsons threatened, "We're in the gang and live next door."

"Next door but one." Rosie corrected.

"Yes, next door but one, but we're in the gang."

"You three can come for nowt as well then, alright?"

They nodded. So far Rosie and Margaret's show was bankrupt at the box office, and they were now relying heavily on strangers to patronise their careers.

"When is the show then?" Alan Thompson asked.

"Tomorrow afternoon," Rosie replied.

"What time?"

"After dinner, 12 o'clock."

"We don't have our dinner till half-past twelve," said the Thompsons.

"All right then, 1 o'clock."

"You can't do it at 1 o'clock, my dad's on nights and he doesn't get up till two." Herbert announced.

"Oh, alright then, half past two, is that alright?"

"It's alright by us," we all chorused.

"Good," said Rosie.

Margaret spoke, after first removing her finger; "I can't act at half past two, I have to turn the mangle for my mam at that time, it's washday."

Rosie's frustration was boiling.

"Alright then, you all say a time," she fumed.

"How about half past three?" one Thompson said.

"No good, I've got to fetch my dad his paper then," Barry chimed in.

"Four o'clock then?"

"No good, it's tea time."

"I know," said Herbert, "How about six o'clock?"

We all agreed, six o'clock was ideal, all that is except Rosie.

"I have to take my grandma her tea down to her house at that time."

"Trust you to be a spoilsport, Rosie." Alan Thompson accused.

"I know," said Rosie, brightening considerably, "I can pretend to take her her tea but come here!"

"What about your grandma's tea?"

"Oh she'll be alright, she can't get out of the house to tell on me, so nobody'll know."

And so it was agreed; The Rosie and Margaret Show would open at six o'clock sharp the following day.

"Emily, Emily what's all these bleeding kids doing queueing in the entry outside?" My Uncle George had a neat turn of phrase when confronted with the unusual. "Tell 'em to piss off or I'll set dog on 'em." Uncle George didn't have a dog but the kids in the passage didn't know that.

"Shush Jud, our Margaret's putting on a show."

"What again! Where's my tea? Bloody show! It's about time she grew up."

"Jud, you were a kid yourself once, remember?"

"Aye and I didn't put on bleeding daft shows! Lasses, I can't understand them."

We all stood behind Uncle George's hut until he was safely inside the house. "Did you hear that? The entry's full of kids for the show." Rosie whispered in an excited breath.

"What's in the basin, Rosie?" one of the Thompsons asked.

"It's my grandma's tea."

"What is it?"

"Stew an' dumplings."

"Give us some."

She removed the greaseproof paper and we demolished her grandmother's tea. When the basin was empty Barry complained, "It were cold."

"I've been here an hour," said Rosie. "You'd be cold if you'd been in a basin an hour."

"Come on let's do the show."

The afternoon had been spent erecting the stage; what that meant was pulling up all the weeds that were over six inches high, removing an old bicycle frame and finding Uncle Jud's garden rake, lost last year. We'd stretched the clothes line across from the hook set in the lavatory wall, and tied it to the leaning clothes post. Across this had been draped an old blackout curtain. We were quite pleased with the result. The dustbin was placed behind the curtain and Alan Thompson had volunteered to be the drummer for the show. Barry was at the gate, ready to collect the halfpennies as the audience filed in. Herbert and me acted as usherettes, bullying infants into their seats. Soon the yard was packed with kids of all sizes. Sisters shushed their charges. Brothers thumped sisters. Mayhem reigned.

"Emily, for Christ's sake, what's that row?"

"Shush, Jud, it's the audience for the show."

"Bleeding show! Yard's like a pippy show! Fetch our Margaret here."

"Leave her Jud, they're only playing."

"Christ Almighty."

Barry, the money safely in his pocket, slipped behind the curtain. "Are you ready?" he hissed at Rosie. "Not yet, we're putting our make-up on,' she hissed back.

The make-up was self-raising flour for powder and the dye from a red liquorice torpedo for lipstick. Both Rosie and Margaret looked very anaemic.

"Hurry up, they're waiting."

"We're ready now."

Barry stood behind the curtain and using his kazoo blew a fanfare. The audience continued to chatter and cry.

"Louder," Rosie called, "They didn't hear you!" The fanfare sounded again.

"Listen! Show's going to start," someone called.

The audience hushed and eyes riveted on the curtain.

"Announce us now," whispered Rosie. Barry crawled under the curtain and stood up.

"Ladies and genklemen. The show is just going to start now and in it is Rosie Bacon who dances and walks on a tight rope across the stage to the other side on her own. After she's done that our Margaret, I mean Margaret Butler, is going to sing a song from the wireless and whistle an' all. She's a good whistler, I taught her. After that, Alan Thompson will play the drums for you on the bin and sing a cowboy song on his own what he's learnt. I don't do owt but introduce them all when you've finished clapping them after they've done their acts. Thank you."

His speech over, Barry crawled back under the curtain.

"They're ready for you now," he said to Rosie.

Rosie and Margaret began to giggle. "I'm not going out there," Margaret said.

"Oh, come on," urged Rosie, pushing and pulling Margaret.

"Pull the curtain back Barry, " Rosie commanded.

With a great swish, and a breaking of clothes line, the curtain collapsed to reveal both girls struggling, down stage, left.

"I'm not going to do it, I'm not!" Margaret trembled.

"Alright, I'll go on first," Rosie conceded and let go Margaret who dashed off to hide behind the hut.

Rosie walked to centre stage, threw her head back, and spoke, "Ladies and genklemen, I would like to sing a song for you called *Maisy dowts and dozzy dowts* what I heard on the wireless."

Alan Thompson started to beat the daylights out of the dustbin with a poker.

"Not yet, not yet," Rosie spun round on him, 'I haven't finished talking yet." Alan stopped.

"Emily! What's that bleeding noise outside?" Uncle George roared.

"I don't know Jud. Probably it's kids."

"Bleeding kids! Where's my cap, I'm going to the lav."

Uncle George's trips to the lavatory were legendary. Precisely at six thirty each evening he donned his cap, folded the newspaper, tucked it under his arm, and proceeded to the lavatory in the yard, there to do the necessary and to read for one hour. This night was no exception. He opened the kitchen door and a deathly hush fell over the assembled mass. He stood momentarily staring at the sea of scruffy faces, then muttering under his breath, he walked to the lavatory door, snecked it open and went in. Every pair of eyes followed his progress; every pair of lungs held their breath until the door closed.

"As I were saying..." said Rosie and all eyes returned to her, "As I were saying, I am now going to sing."

From inside the lav came a noise like thunder. All the audience collapsed in hysterics.

Uncle George's voice boomed from behind the door, "Piss off, before I come out and clip you!"

There were stifled giggles then quiet. Rosie started her song. Alan started his drumming. Uncle George started raving.

"Shut up you little sods! Can't a bloke read his paper in peace!"

Rosie spoke, "I will now stop my singing, ladies and genklemen, and do my tight rope walking act across the stage."

There was a muffled; "Thank God for that," from behind the lavatory door.

"I shall call on my assistant to put up my special tight rope walking rope, thank you."

Barry moved forward, bowed, and proceeded to tie a piece of old clothes line to the clothes post. He stretched it tight and fastened the other end to the lavatory door handle. This done, he made to leave the stage.

Rosie hissed, "Introduce me, you burk."

Barry turned, looked surprised, and said; "Oh yer." He

stepped forward. "Ladies and genklemen, Rosie is now going to walk on the tight rope for you. Her dad learnt to do it in the army where he were fighting the Germans that he beat and got a medal for what's in their house, Rosie says." He bowed and left.

Rosie now saw the size of her task and her mind raced for an excuse.

"Ladies and genklemen, the rope is too high for me."

Barry adjusted it until it stretched two feet from the ground.

"Thank you," quavered Rosie.

The gang was now very interested. Could she, after all, tight rope walk? Rosie took a step towards the line. We held our breath. She stood on an upturned bucket, her arms outstretched, looking for all the world as though she knew what she was doing. Alan Thompson attacked the dust bin once again. Rosie placed a foot on the line; it sagged. She wobbled, her other foot still on the bucket.

"Come on Rosie, you can do it." Barry shouted.

She stumbled and fell. the audience gave a scornful gasp.

"Ladies and genklemen," she addressed them, "I'm sorry about that, but that burk put me off shouting. I shall try again and keep thee gob shut."

Once more Rosie stood on the bucket. Once more her foot stretched the line. Once more the bin was punished. Suddenly her full weight was pressing the rope down. Quickly she ran along it as it lay on the grass. There was a twang, and the lavatory door handle shot off.

There were cries of "Cheat! Rubbish! Give us us money back!"

Barry was screaming with laughter.

Rosie was shouting above the din, "I did it! I did it! Did you see me? I tight rope walked like I said I would!"

"You didn't! You walked on the ground! It's a cheat, give us us money back!"

"I'm going to fetch my mam if you don't let us have our money."

"But the show's not over" Rosie protested, "Margaret's not sung yet, and I've not tap danced for you."

"Give us us money back! We want our money back!"

"Alright, alright! Take your money an' none of you are coming to a show any more," Rosie shouted bitterly.

They crowded around Barry, who delved deep into his grubby pockets to return the pennies and halfpennies. The audience filed up the entry and out onto the street, dispersing to their various homes.

We stood in the deserted yard looking at Rosie.

"I did do it! I did, didn't I?" Rosie sobbed.

"Course you did Rosie, we all saw you, didn't we?"

"Come on let's go play on the bomb site!"

The yard emptied.

In the lavatory Uncle George slumbered on. The newspaper lay neglected on the floor. A daddy long legs casually walked across the headlines. All was quiet. It was the sudden lack of noise that woke him. He sat and stretched and then, with a sigh, he stood and pulled his trousers up. The clunk of the flush heralded his ritual over and he felt automatically for the door's inside sneck. It was missing. He stood, braces dangling, a puzzled look on his stubbly face. He pushed the door, it didn't budge. He pushed harder. Still no movement.

He called softly; "Hello. Hello. Anybody there?" Silence. "I said hello, is anybody there?"

"Emily! Emily! I'm locked in the lav! Emily, come and open the door! Emily! Stop messing about! Come and open the bleeding door!"

Auntie Em sat sipping a cup of tea and having a good old natter with Mrs Lindley. They were putting the world to rights and the neighbours to wrongs. The time slipped by until eventually Auntie stood and said, "I'll have to be going love, I'll have to get Barry and Margaret in for bed."

At half past nine Auntie Em made a cup of tea and for the first time that night wondered where Jud was.

"Gone to the pub I expect," she muttered. "Oh well, I think I'll turn in." Her trip down the yard before retiring was obligatory. She approached the lavatory door and it was then she heard strange noises issuing from within. Someone was in the lav! She plucked up courage, the call of nature screaming at her.

'Hello. Hello. Who's in there? You'd better come out, I've got my husband with me!"

A voice from within. "You've got your husband with you, have you? Well, who the bleeding hell am I then? You silly sod! Get this door open quick!"

"Jud! Is that you in there?"

"Course it is, woman!"

"Just a minute love!"

"Don't love me you silly bleeder, open the door! Four

hours I've been stuck in here! Where have you been?"

"Mrs Lindley's."

"Christ! I'm stuck in here an' she's gobbing off at old lass Lindley's! Get this door open quick!"

She pulled at the sneck and the door creaked open.

"Thank Christ for that!" said Uncle George, emerging into the night air.

He looked bedraggled and his clothes were covered in white wash from the walls. A spider sat on his shoulder.

"How did you get stuck in there?" Auntie wanted to know.

"Sneck broke you silly cow! I'll fix it tomorrow. I'm going to bed."

He walked into the darkness, leaving Auntie Em to find her own way back. She sat on the lav with a smirk on her face.

*

During the war food was scarce. Not that we kids noticed it — what we'd never had we never missed. Bread and scran, margarine, was normal food. So was chips. One day a large box arrived at our house, mum opened it up, her face wreathed in smiles. Inside were packages and tins; tinned peaches, tinned pears, all sorts. There was a tall, waxy, carton with the American flag and an eagle on it. It looked really colourful — out of this world. All we saw of packets were rare blue sugar bags, greaseproof paper and brown paper bags. Inside this exotic carton was dried egg powder and proper jelly packets, not the articifial stuff which mum tried bravely to make set and disguise the taste of. Mum displayed all the goods on the cellar head. Now and then we'd go and open the door just to gaze at the pictures of large round fruit on the labels. The tinned fruit and the dried currants and raisins were to be saved for Christmas, mum told us, but the dried egg powder was used to make fabulous omelettes and scrambled egg. Mum made egg custard that melted in your mouth.

Dad was a good cook in a rough and ready sort of way. His fried corned beef was delicious and his 'Johnny Curnudgeits' were spot on. 'Johnny Curnudgeits' was corned beef laid on the bottom of a dish, slices of onion on top and sliced potatoes on top of the onions. Gravy was poured over the whole and it was placed in the coal oven to cook. Mum's stuffed roast rabbit was a rare treat, and her baked bread great. With the spare dough Herbert and I made gingerbread-men, not ginger really but that's what we called them. We used currants for eyes, nose, and the buttons down the front of the coat, and placed them on the oven bottom to cook. When they were ready, we'd cannibalise them, eating the head, then the arms and legs. The hot bread tasted of whatever dirt it had cleaned from our grubby hands and the currants were as hard as bullets.

Mum also made a kind of cheese for herself, which no-one else liked. If the milk curdled she'd pour it into one of her stockings, then hang it over the sink so that the whey could drip out. She relished it and called it clotted cheese; it smelt like sour milk to us, but mum liked it.

VE night signalled the end of the war and street parties were held all over Sheffield. It meant the end of the blackout, people left lights on in their houses and the curtains drawn back in a relieved defiance. Our street party was great. Long trestle tables were set up down the middle of the road, and we ate our way through all sorts of goodies. Rationing was still in force but mums did wonders with what little they had. Dads erected a massive bonfire a little way up the road and at dusk it was lit. The flames leapt as high as the roof tops as we played around it. The tar between the cobbles melted and ran into the fire. We threw potatoes into the white hot embers and after a while prodded them out with sticks. The black, burnt spuds were eaten along with mouthfuls of charcoal. Dads manhandled Mrs Lindley's great radiogram out onto the pavement, and as soon as electricity was had from Uncle George's front room ceiling socket, music blasted and echoed around the roofs, rattling the loose window panes. They danced and drank well into the night. We ate and played with the fire until we could hardly keep our eyes open.

The following morning the pile of white ash still smouldered and broke into flames at the least breeze. We played with it for a while but soon wandered off in search of something different to do. V.E. night was over and things were pretty much the same, no visible difference at all. We'd imagined soldiers marching defeated Germans up our road at least, but nothing at all. What an anticlimax. No more sleeping in the shelter, no more sirens or dad telling mum what Mr Churchill was going to do the following week.

With the end of the war things started to creep back into the shops, if you had money. The first time I saw a banana was at school. During playtime Harry Churchyard pulled it from his pocket and proudly showed off the bright yellow fruit to the gathered crowd. We wondered what it was. His brother who was in the navy had brought some bananas home with him on leave. Harry peeled it and broke it into as many pieces as he could for handing around to us. The taste was out of this world. The only fruits we knew were apples, the occasional orange and a long dried, dark brown polished object, called lotus fruit. When broken in two it smelled of something unmentionable. When eaten it was sickly sweet, far sweeter than sugar, and left an after taste that lingered for hours.

Nothing could rid that taste from our mouths, except, perhaps, liquorice root, which could be bought from the local corner shop. We always hoped for the thick stumpy pieces, more flavour you see; the thin long pieces turned bitter and splintered too easily in our yellow-stained mouths. We'd chew and chew the root wood until all the bittersweet flavour was extracted and the wood reduced to pulp then, spitting it out, wish we hadn't had it. It left a taste in the mouth like the smell of gas.

When word went round that the corner shop had 'crystals', off we'd go and buy a halfpennyworth of them. Poured into a cone shaped bag, they smelled strongly of lemons. Fingers soon became bright yellow, as did tongues and lips. We hit on the idea of making fizzy drinks from them and experimented using baking powder for fizz and the crystals for taste. It was foul, but we drank it and burped our way through the day, feeling rather sick and bloated.

*

The winter of 1947 was heralded in for us early one morning as we lay in bed. Dad woke us up, smiling over us. In his hand he held a snowball. For a moment it didn't register then, as understanding pushed its way through our sleep ridden heads, we jumped out of bed onto the cold boards and pulling back the curtains stared out into wonderland. Had it snowed? I'll say. In the night it must have thrown the stuff down. The dustbin had disappeared under the white glistening blanket. On the sloping lavatory roof it lay some twelve inches deep, and it was still falling thick and heavy.

Great flakes, some two inches across, tumbled and twisted to add to the already deep covering.

Dressed, and downstairs, we gobbled our porridge. The light in the room was still on because of the dark, lowering sky that steadily shed its white load. Mum said we could go out when it stopped. It didn't, and at bedtime, peeping through the window we watched it bury the clothes post in our tiny patch of a garden. Dad was working nights at the steelworks. We watched him pull on his overcoat and muffler as mum put his packing up in his knapsack. We envied him being able to go out in the snow. At nine o'clock he set off to battle his way to work. We had cocoa and went to bed. The oven plate was in so we were soon snuggled down to dream of the weather outside. It snowed all night.

The following day dawned blindingly bright. Outside it had stopped snowing. All sounds were muffled and dull. the enormously thick blanket had evened out all the humps and hollows. The wind that had followed the clouds began to drift the snow into great knife edged curves. The road had lost all semblance of ever having existed apart from the cross bars of the gaslamps. We were snowed in.

Dad's homecoming was greeted with great excitement. He'd battled his way home, starting at seven o'clock, and arrived exhausted at ten. He got his shovel from the hut and had to dig his way to the back door to gain entry. Sitting by the fire, thawing out, he answered all our excited questions. Mum fed him a good breakfast, fussing over him, until finally warmed through, he ascended the stairs to bed. We muffled up warm and, pulling on our wellies, ventured out into the white world. We had great fun digging our way to the lavatory. We dug a track just for fun, snaking it around the garden. Pretty soon, our private snow was trampled and its pristine neatness gone. Off we set up the entry in search of virgin public snow out on the road. There were great drifts everywhere and we dug into them with enthusiasm, fashioning caves and hollows, tunnels and shafts. Some collapsed in on us burying our sweating bodies. We clawed our way out, laughing between mouthfuls of snow, tasting the cold powdery stuff tingling our tongues.

What a winter! It went on and on. Temperatures well below zero at all times. The outside toilet froze solid, so did the kitchen taps. Every morning the windows had newly designed lace curtains frozen there from the internal condensation. The coal ran out and the coal man couldn't deliver; we foraged for anything that would burn. We heard tales of people pulling their floorboards up and of others chopping up their furniture for fuel.

Uncle George dismantled his garden hut a piece at a time to burn; the very hut he'd built so proudly the previous summer. Slowly us kids began to get fed up with the eternal cold and went outside less and less until it was rare to see anyone outside that didn't have to be. We grew miserable tied to the house. Mum grew short tempered with us always under her feet. Dad was really tired out tramping to work, then at night ensuring the following day's supply of fire wood.

Then one day it was thawing. The gutters were dripping slowly but nevertheless the splash was the proof. As quickly as the snows had come they left. The solid ice on the roads proved stubborn but the corporation workmen came and melted it with great roaring burners. That summer was a scorcher.

*

Harry Churchyard came to stay with his auntie and was soon hanging around trying to join our gang. Now, our gang was exclusive and outsiders were not welcome, so said Rosie Bacon. But one day when we were playing on the flat part, Harry revealed some fascinating information that made even Rosie have second thoughts.

"My dad's just got demobbed," he announced from a safe distance away at the edge of the bombed site. We pretended not to notice him.

"My dad's brought his bayonet home with him."

We glanced at each other. A bayonet.

Barry shouted across to him "You can join the gang if you get it and show it us."

Harry's face dropped. "He keeps it locked up."

"Clear off then."

We continued to play. Harry hung around, seeking inspiration.

"My dad fought with the Jerkers."

"What's Jerkers?" one of the Thompsons shouted.

"If I tell you can I join the gang?"

We put our heads together. "Let's find out about the Jerkers then sod him off," we agreed.

"Come over here and tell us."

He scrambled through the rubbish to us.

"What's your name?" Rosie asked.

"Harry Churchyard, and I'm tough."

We laughed.

"What's a Jerker then? Come on tell us." Barry menaced.

And so it was that we found out about the Ghurkas. Harry told us how he'd heard his mother telling his auntie what his dad had told his mother.

"They're a tribe who live in the jungle. They're black and tough. This explorer found them living in a swamp; he showed them a photo of our King and they thought he looked smart in his crown so they said they'd fight forever for him.

"They've got a knife each, it's called a cuckoo. Thing is, if they take it out of its sheath they've got to draw blood before they can put it back."

We were enthralled, he'd got us.

"Honest?" asked Rosie.

"True, mother die if I'm lying.

"Every time they clean it they have to cut their arms for blood."

"Wow!" said Alan Thompson, "Let's form a Jerker regiment!"

"We'll call our knives cuckoos and draw blood with them."

In the heat of the moment we all agreed and Harry joined the gang. We didn't know any jungle talk apart from Paul Robeson, who we'd seen in the film *Saunders Of The River* and *Sabu, the Elephant Boy*, in his films. This didn't limit us and the for the next two weeks we ended every sentence with either 'i-e-o-coe,' or 'simba.'

The cleaning of the cuckoos was fraught with danger and suddenly everybody's knives, which we kept razor sharp on the kerbstones, became so blunt that they wouldn't have cut butter. Everybody had an excuse when forced to use their weapons. Tommy Turner inadvertently nicked his finger while sharpening a piece of wood. The blood flow was minute but he played it up.

"I'm safe to put my cuckoo away now," he announced, grandly.

We were envious and he goaded us all day, squeezing his finger to keep the blood flowing.

The Ghurkas soon lost their popularity in the gang, so did Harry Churchyard. The excuse came when Barry overheard his dad talking about "That bloody clever bugger, Churchyard, who'd spent the war at Catterick behind a desk."

Harry didn't show the following day and the Jerkers fell from favour and disappeared into the jungle of our minds.

Weekdays were spent playing games in the street; marbles were favourite. What a collection I had! They were like jewels. Just to hold them and feel their round, glassy smoothness was the most satisfying feeling I knew; they were precious. Pitches would spring up all along the street; a small hole was gouged out where the paving stones joined. Squatting in a head touching circle we played our hearts out. No finger pushing or 'cabbaging' was allowed on pain of a thump. We never played with our best 'mabs', they were far too good and were reserved for trading.

Cigarette cards were another hobby. I had a few sets and once an uncle gave me a biscuit tin full of assorted cards, including some silk ones.

Bubble bursting was a popular pastime. The sun beat down on the cobblestones and melted the tar between, raising it up into soft, shiny bubbles. It was very soothing to lie in the road and slowly pop the black spheres.

Enoch sat in the tyre which hung by a rope from the arm of a gas lamp while the rest of the gang lay in the road collecting the warm tar into handsized balls to mould into tar babies. We watched as a black car halted outside the corner shop on the opposite side of the road. Mr Chippinghouse, our local corner shop grocer, applied the handbrake, looked through the passenger window. saw the gang, and muttered as he swung his door forward and open.

"Little bleeders."

"Hello Mr Chippinghouse," Rosie shouted, "I like yer new motor car."

"Keep yer bloody hands off it, you little swines," he answered.

"Is it a Ford?" Enoch shouted, as Brian gave him the sixth push of his rationed ten swings.

Mr Chippinghouse ignored the question, spotted a minute speck of dust on the bonnet, bent, blew it away, straightened, and repeated his request, "Don't you buggers dare touch it or I'll skin you alive."

"It's not as good as the insurance man's," Enoch shouted. "His is a Morris."

Mr Chippinghouse clenched his fists and wished the swinging rope would break and maim Enoch for daring to compare his car with the car of a menial, who wasn't even self-employed. In his heart he knew Enoch's statement was true and this only served to make the comment even more bitter to live with.

"I'm warning you lot, don't dare come near it or I'll murder you!"

Mr Chippinghouse closed the car door, turned, and with the germ of dissatisfaction now festering within his small mind, determined to add a penny to the price of all his goods, thus ensuring sufficient profits to purchase a Morris the following spring. The shop door slammed shut, rattling the shop window and toppling a display pyramid of donkey stones.

At the extreme arc of his swing, Enoch glanced towards the shop, smirked, and was satisfied that he still possessed the innate knack of fraying people's nerve endings.

The tyre swinging session came to an end abruptly when Police Constable Neville King rounded the bottom of the street and allowed his chrome leather boots to proceed up the worn pavement towards the hastily peaceful gang who now sat on the kerb edge opposite Mr Chippinghouse's parked car. He steadily approached us, and with each step we became increasingly preoccupied in bursting the tar bubbles. The sound of studs steadily being worn away ceased, and we all sensed the blue tower of the law looking at our bent backs.

"And what have we here?" a deep voice sounded.

We all turned, and with heads at right angles to our shoulders, stared up into the distant face that looked down on us.

"Hello Mr King," Brian said.

Rosie nudged him sharply with her elbow. "You don't say *Mister* when Mr King is in his crime outfit, you say Constable King," she hissed.

"Oh sorry Mr King," Brian said, "I should have said Constable King, Rosie says."

Constable King smiled inwardly. "That's alright son," he answered, "How's your mother's back, Rosie?"

"It's a lot better now, thank you," Rosie said politely. "Me dad says Doctor Mackintosh has worked miracles since she's been under him."

PC King hooked a finger into the chin strap of his helmet, and easing the thin leather, smiled wryly.

"Can you show us your truncheon, Constable King? Like you did last time?" Enoch asked.

"I think that can be arranged," PC King replied, and with a great show of lifting the side of his tunic, he withdrew the heavily polished queller of the masses, "Here we are."

"Wow!" Enoch gasped, "I bet that hurts if you cop it on yer nut."

"Well, if you don't ever do anything wrong, I won't have to put it to the test, will I, young Enoch?"

Enoch shook his head.

"Have you caught any criminals today?" Alan ventured to ask.

"No, not yet," he replied good naturedly. "Why have you seen any?" Automatically we all glanced to Mr Chippinghouse's corner shop. After all, charging tuppence for liquorice root, well surely that was a crime, and his lemonade crystals were now priced well out of reach of our spending money, which incidently we never received.

"N..n..no, I don't think so," Rosie replied. "Although somebody has pinched the seat from Mrs Brigham's lavatory."

Enoch dropped his head and played with the tar bubbles in earnest. "She's got a big gob," he thought. "Hope he doesn't investigate and find out it was me."

"That seems a strange thing to steal," PC King said.

"He obviously doesn't know how cold a pot bowl is first thing in the morning," Enoch thought, "If me dad hadn't chopped ours up for the fire, I wouldn't now be on the verge of receiving a clobbering from a copper's truncheon." He sighed inwardly and wondered why, of all his family, only he appreciated the little luxuries in life.

"Well, kids," PC King said as he replaced his truncheon, "I must be on my way, be good, I'll call at Mrs Brigham's later."

He turned, faced his bulk towards the top of the street, straightened his tunic, adjusted his helmet, and strode off with measured, size twelve steps.

Mr Chippinghouse watched from behind his rebuilt donkey stone display and cursed PC King for not arresting all the little varmints and ridding the neighbourhood of the sounds of children laughing and playing. Turning, he entered his rear stockroom, and using a salted cloth, began wiping maggots from the side of bacon that hung from the sagging ceiling. As he worked he made a mental note to sort out the mouse droppings from the bag of bulk sugar which he had purchased from a shady character earlier in the week. Mr Chippinghouse was nothing if not industrious.

When Enoch and the rest of us had collected enough tar to make a tar baby, we stood, and as if drawn by a magnet, we sidled across the road towards Mr Chippinghouse's sparklingly clean car.

"It shines dun't it?" Alan said.

We all nodded in agreement. Rosie bent to peer through the wing mirror. Finding it was at the wrong angle, she reached, and grasping the chrome fitting, pulled it until her reflection stared back at her. The chrome was now coated in road tar.

"It makes yer face look right small," she informed the gang. Soon we were all taking turns to test the truth of her statement.

"If yer get right close to it, yer nose looks massive," Brian laughed.

He reached to the mirror and watched his finger end grow to enormous proportions. When he withdrew it a perfect tar finger print remained.

Herbert innocently added his portion of tar by copying Brian. Meanwhile Enoch had moulded his ball of tar into a miniature baby and now glanced around for somewhere to test its standing capabilities. The somewhere he chose was the nearside mud guard. He stood back and admired the mannequin which he had fathered, then watched as it slowly toppled to one side and slid down the length of the gleaming paint work, leaving an immovable streak of sticky tar in its wake. Enoch sniffed, then lost interest as his eye was caught by a blue and chrome badge that was sitting proudly on the front bumper.

"Look at this!" he called to the others. We all bent and peered at the badge.

"RAC" Margaret spelt out, "What's that mean?"

Brian thought for a moment then announced, "Rotten Albert Chippinghouse."

We all laughed.

"It's smart though, isn't it?" Herbert said, and caressed the smooth metal.

"You've put tar on it now," Rosie exclaimed.

"It'll wash off," Herbert answered. "It's only a bit of tar."

Mrs Lindley's ginger cat strolled towards the rear off-side wheel, jerkily sniffed at the rubber, turned with its back to it, and dosed it thoroughly.

"I wonder why cats always tiddle backwards?" Barry asked as we watched the cat's performance with academic interest.

"Probably God made a mistake and put their thingies on the wrong way," Enoch replied.

We all giggled.

"That's daft," Rosie said. "He could have," Enoch defended, "I mean how many times have you heard us mams say our dads have got eyes in the back of their heads? Same thing in't it?"

High in the smoky blue sky, a rubbish tip seagull winged its way towards its evening roost, wishing it hadn't eaten the contents of a discarded tin of mouldy green corned beef. It's stomach rumbled and bubbled uncontrollably. With a painful cry, nature took over, and Mr Chippinghouse's car roof was decorated with a star shaped, paint dissolving pattern.

The gang sauntered around to the off-side, where Margaret sat on the running board, watching her image in the polished paint work as she studiously picked her nose.

"We're going to the bomb site, are you coming?" Rosie asked. Margaret removed her finger and nodded a yes. Reaching to the door handle, she hoisted herself to her feet, and in the process coated the chrome with more tar. She stood, eased the knicker elastic which was cutting into her, and followed the innocent despoilers of new things as they walked up the street towards the ruins.

*

I was in the Cubs. St Alban's troop. We met every Monday night in the Church Hall and dibbed and dobbed and Arkelaed to our hearts' content, learning knots and semaphore and getting as many badges as possible. House Orderly, Joinery, Cooking, Knots, First Aid and dozens of others adorned the sleeves of my itchy blue jersey.

Eventually I attained the rank of senior sixer and with it my own cub pack. We marched the streets at the drop of a hat. Any excuse and St Alban's would parade, four abreast, the Scouts up front, followed by the Cubs, followed by the Guides, followed by the Brownies, followed by a straggly lot who couldn't make their minds up as to joining, or were simply there to take the mickey and giggle.

Everyone aspired to join the band. The thrill of banging your own personal drum or blowing a battered, polished trumpet — it was every Cub's dream!

Herbert had his trumpet for some time as he was in the Scouts. And then, one day, I was given a side drum. Practising at home was hell for mum. We were relegated to the empty front room to bang and blow with carefree abandon. Next door, Mrs Brigham's hens stopped laying from sheer fright. Learning rolls was hard but eventually I mastered them. I quickly picked up the various beats with Herbert's help and I awaited Sunday Church Parade with eagerness.

We lined up outside the church at eight thirty on Sunday morning and when it was deemed time, off we marched. The narrow streets echoed to our crashing, each drummer trying to outdo his companion — to the distress of all those still in bed after a good night on the beer. The trumpets were sheer out-of-tune murder. I bet a few heads throbbed at our passing. If the Salvation Army happened to be playing on a corner as we passed we'd increase the cacophony, delighting in drowning their polished silver sounds.

"Keep it down lads, keep it down," Arkela shouted above the row, his hairy knees wobbling as they carried his bulk onwards in front of the mayhem. Our eyes glinted with the beat. We were like demons, possessed. On we thumped up March Street, down Jubilee Road and along Greenland Road, the parade stretching out behind us. We banged our way all round Darnall then back to the church for Morning Service. Trooping inside, our ears deaf and our arms aching, we sat watching Mr Frieze, the German vicar, mouthing his silent sermon to our indifferent ears.

Going to camp once a year was exciting. For weeks before, we packed and unpacked our kitbags, rehearsing our equipment for the great day. When it arrived, we staggered off under our enormous burdens to the Church Hall. The lorry that was to take us was parked outside, its tail board down, receiving kit bags, rucksacks, carrier bags, anything that could hold clothes and personal possessions. After it was loaded we scrambled aboard, plonking ourselves down amongst the heap. We sang the journey away with *One Man*

Went To Mow, *Ten Green Bottles*, and *Underneath The Spreading Chestnut Tree*. Passing through the impressive gates of Wellbeck Abbey, the lorry trundled through the spacious grounds to our allotted camp site. Enormous army bell tents were erected, pitch black inside and smelling as only heavy waterproof canvas can. The heat built up all day as the sun beat down, and at night it was an oven, housing thirty sunburnt Scouts, snoring their heads off. All feet pointed to the centre pole, all in great quilted ex-Army sleeping bags, looking like green caterpillars.

*

To catch a cold was a rare thing. The soot and the sulphur in the air from the smoky chimneys must have choked most germs, but at the first hint of a snuffle dad would say; "He wants his chest rubbing."

Dad's favourite chest rubbing ointment was goose grease straight from the roasting pan. He scooped it up with his fingers and while we held shirts up to necks, he rubbed the grease hard into our skin with coarse, calloused hands. If we yelled out he'd say; "It's doing you good son, this'll get rid of your cold."

Failing goose grease, his second favourite was camphorated oil. That smelled better than dead duck's fat, and didn't attract the dogs as much. It also had that special mystique of being purchased from the chemist's. After hard rubbing, back and front, a smear was applied under our noses and around our throats then off to bed. Sore throats were treated with the magical sweaty sock. Dad would pin one of his socks around the affected throat and it was worn all night. Earache was treated in a special way; mum boiled an onion and, when cooked, the centre sliver was put in the ear and held in place with a bandage. The pain was excruciating. You had to be tough to survive, in those days. For colds we swallowed a teaspoonful of Vick's Vapour Rub, clogging the nostrils with it for a head cold. Then there was the famous, or was it infamous, bread poultice; boiling bread, sandwiched between muslin, and applied to a boil on the back of the neck. Sheer torture this, but endured, because always the famous phrase; "It'll do you good son" rang out.

*

School was Phillimore Infants and Junior School; sitting at desk all day, being bullied at playtime and being bullied by teachers with the threat of cane or slipper. Blackboard rubbers or chalk were thrown at inattentive heads and your knuckles were rapped for minor misdemeanours. Dinners consisted of lumps of yellow fat in stew.

School to me meant respecting the 'cock of the class' or challenging him to a fight, after lessons, behind the playground toilets. Phillimore Road School was a tough grounding in life, but it certainly knocked the corners off us.

The three 'Rs' were drummed in. Everyone left able to read and write — albeit with bruised hands. Physical training was carried out in the school hall-cum-gym-cum-dinner hall-cum-assembly hall. Our instructor was merciless. If you couldn't clear the vaulting horse a rubber slipper on the backside helped you over the next time. We achieved fitness by avoiding the slipper.

Assembly was held each morning at a quarter to nine. We had to march in, holding hands, to the tempo of *Country Garden*. We stood in lines, sang a short hymn, garbled a prayer and listened as the Headmaster cursed "Whoever it was who had blocked the playground toilets with two miles of Izal toilet paper and was too cowardly to come forward." Teachers, in the meantime patrolled the lines, aching to find a wrongdoer. This over, we'd march out to the same tune to our respective classes.

The teachers called us by surname. The pupils called the teacher 'Sir' or 'Miss' incessantly; the more frightened we were the more 'Sirs' to a sentence. When the students from the university arrived, those taking up the teaching and beating profession, it was great. They were still bright-eyed and bushy-tailed, and so we took advantage. When they left it was back to dodging the rubber and chalk.

"The Nit Nurse is coming after playtime," Alan Thompson said casually, throwing a piece of loose tarmac at a small, undernourished, reluctant seeker of knowledge and effectively maiming him.

We watched absentmindedly as he hobbled off with tears streaming down his face to find solace from his older sister.

"That were a bit cruel," Barry said.

"No, it wasn't," Alan replied. "He should have dodged it."

"How could he dodge it?" Brian exclaimed, "he didn't

even see it was coming."

"That were his fault," Alan sniffed.

"And this is my fault, Thompson." An adult voice sounded behind us.

Mr Mitchell's scutches were legendary, and Alan experienced first hand the pain caused by one.

"See me after school, Thompson," he commanded.

"Yes sir," Alan mumbled, clutching the back of his head.

Mr Mitchell walked away sucking on his school whistle.

"I'll tell my dad on him," Alan muttered, knowing he wouldn't. Parents always agreed with teachers.

Mr Mitchell's whistle sounded, and we formed into our lines ready to march back into the high security block called Phillimore Junior and Infants School.

Our class faced south and suffered under the sun all day. Miss Fillibut snecked the door open, took her last breath of fresh air from the corridor, entered, and as usual gagged, as the wall of odour enveloped her.

"Right children," she retched, "The school nurse is here. As your names are called, form up in the corridor." Phillimore Road School was obsessed with hygiene. Finger nail inspection every day and the occasional visit by the school nurse. She was a giant of a woman whose starched white uniform swelled to bursting point over her gigantic breasts.

We trooped into the makeshift clinic and stood awaiting our turn to be examined. Heads were thrust between her mounds and, approaching suffocation, we were inspected for nits. She'd pull and tug at the roots, searching for the little demons.

"I haven't got any, miss" we'd protest, "Me mam sees to them."

But it fell on deaf ears, she'd search anyway. She also looked up our noses, down our throats, in our ears; in fact she'd peer into any opening that presented itself. If any scabs were in evidence she produced a great brown bottle of purple liquid and liberally coated the area. One by one we were camouflaged with the purple liquid and when we were all treated, we marched back to our sun baked classroom, to loll and carve desks into masterpieces of renaissance art.

We also had tonsil inspection. Your tongue was pushed down hard with a wooden stick and a torch was shone down your throat. Pity the poor soul who had a bit of a sore throat at the time. Off he was sent, via a form to his mother, to the hospital to have his tonsils out, pacified with promises of loads of ice cream.

Teeth were inspected intermittently; if one needed attention we were sent home with a note and a form for our parents to give permission. Much to my dismay, mum always signed my teeth away and on the allotted day, dragged me to the clinic. The clinic was a single-storey wooden building without curtains. Inside, it was all green and brown paint with a few cheery posters of gaping mouths in various stages of decay. On long wooden forms arranged in the main room sat head-scarfed mothers, with terrified sons or daughters, pale-faced and trembling. Periodically, names were called and a mother would stand and escort her off-spring to the closed, glass-panelled door that led to the extraction room. The nearer it got to my turn the more fear pumped into my brain until, sweating and stiff, I was pulled through that hateful door.

Down a short corridor was another door, half open, through which I could hear whimpering and crying. Mum dragged me into a brightly-lit room. In the centre stood a black padded chair, gas cylinders at its side. The air reeked of a sweet smell which made me feel sick as mum forced me into the chair. I was struggling and had to be held down as a great, stinking, rubber mask descended on to my face.

I cried out and fought wildly. The smell was sickeningly overpowering, I fought and fought... but the train flew on down the track, the bright sunlight showing everything crystal clear. On it raced, its wheels banging loudly in my ears, on and on until suddenly a terrific bang, which rocked and burned me and mum said, "Come on love. Walter, come on love, wake up, it's over." My eyes shot open, bright light, Mum bending over me smiling. I was weak and confused, tears rolling down my cheeks, blood tasting in my mouth, a gaping hole felt with my tongue. I cried again, this time with relief. Mum cuddled me to her; dimly I was aware of other children whimpering. Then as reality returned, a feeling of happiness. We walked home with a handkerchief tied over my mouth to keep the cold out. People glanced and smiled. Mum smiled back. At home I was spoilt for a few hours.

When Herbert came home from school he asked "Did it hurt, Walt?"

"No, nothing to it!"

The afternoon wore on. Miss Fillibut was now covering

pond life and the cycle of the Caddis Fly Larva. Why a fly should need a bike was beyond me and I sometimes wondered if Miss Fillibut had enough qualifications to be in charge of our innocent brains.

I glanced across to where Rosie Bacon and Harry Churchyard sat. The heat of the day was stirring deep passions in Rosie, and Harry squirmed in an attempt to stop her writing 'I love you' on the back of his hand with her genuine, imitation, bakelite fountain pen. The course of true love never did run smooth for Rosie, but she was a trier.

We swung into the final phase of our lessons and when the bell sounded, Miss Fillibut changed course in mid stream and without a break in the flow of words began reading us the final chapter of *Treasure Island*, giving a very unconvincing imitation of Long John Silver.

"Arrr, Jim lad, you and me is shipmates," her high pitched, squeaky voice rang out.

My attention level registered minus four after that and I couldn't even conceive of her obtaining a spear-carrying part in the St Alban's Church Drama Group. Besides we'd all seen the film some weeks previously and to form a thought picture of Robert Newton with the voice of Miss Fillibut overtaxed our mental abilities.

At five minutes to four Alan began rubbing cane break mica into his hands to ward off the pain of his coming encounter with Mr Marshall. We all swore by cane break, and swore when it didn't work. Cuthbert Riley had caught Rosie's eye and was mouthing silent questions at her. Rosie was smiling, raising her eyebrows, and nodding "yes" back at him. Another school day was on the verge of collapsing into the vast void of yesterdays.

Suddenly the final bell rang and with a banging of desk lids and crafty thumps into vulnerable backs, we erupted from the classroom into the great outdoors. All, that is, except Alan who began his lonely walk along the cell block towards Mr Marshall's torture chamber. Out in the playground a screaming throng had formed a circle and some luckless hero was endeavouring to beat the 'Cock of the School'. A hopeless task, but one we all brushed up against at frequent intervals. The gang lolled by the toilets awaiting Alan's return and discussing the evening's play. Rosie and Cuthbert were sidling towards the disused air raid shelters to fulfil their previously agreed assignation.

Miss Fillibut, her arms bulging with exercise books containing incorrect answers, ink blots, and gibberish, was climbing into her ancient Ford motor car and heading west towards the rarefied heights of Dore, dreaming of cucumber sandwiches and her tweed clad, hairy husband. Two streets away a factory siren sounded and a great belch of yellow smoke plumed into the summer air to finally settle on backyard washing and donkey stoned steps.

"He's here now," Brian said.

Alan walked from the girls' entrance and crossed to where we were waiting.

"Did it hurt?" Barry asked. Alan nodded.

"What about the cane break, didn't it work?"

"He didn't use the cane, he used a PT plimsol on me backside."

"That's not fair," Brian said indignantly. "We can't rub cane break there."

We stood sympathising with Alan and fuming at the gall of Mr Marshall for daring to break the Geneva Convention regarding animal rights.

The concern for Alan was short lived. After all it was home time and stomachs rumbled for bread and jam. We exited the school playground and wandered towards our street with excitement growing quietly inside at the prospect of the evening's play on the bomb site. Miss Fillibut approached at half a mile an hour, carrying the bulk of Mr Marshall in the passenger seat. The window was down. They drew level.

"Good night children," she squeaked.

"Good night Miss Fillibut, good night Mr Marshall," we chanted.

Alan didn't. Under his breath he whispered, "Sod off Marshall."

Mr Marshall's head shot round and he roared, "Thompson, see me in the morning!"

Alan groaned.

*

Christmas time was a beautiful, exciting, frightening time. It was a combination of weather, feelings and a million other things, mostly abstract, felt not seen. Christmas in summer could never survive. Christmas Eve's magic lay in, "Will he come, mam?"

"What will he bring me?"

"Is it time for bed yet?"

Questions, all met with a non-committal smile from mum who was baking mince pies, jam tarts and lots of other Christmassy things. At bedtime we were scrubbed clean and put in fresh pyjamas. We clutched our starched, cold pillow slips. Upstairs, in bed, we watched mum and dad drawing pin the pillow slips to the rail at the foot of the bed, adding four more holes alongside all the others from past Christmases. Amid excited, nerve-stretched chatter we shot under the clean covers.

"Now settle down you two," mum smiled. "He'll not come if you're awake. No peeking, Walter."

Leaning over us she kissed us, then we felt dad's rough kiss.

"Good night. God bless, sons."

Then we were left alone in the dark to quiver and think and think, trying hard to go to sleep.

For weeks before we'd been writing notes to Father Christmas and despatching them up the smoky chimney. Had he got them? Thoughts tumbled through our minds, picture after picture. I wanted him to come but was frightened of seeing such a powerful, magical person, so I hid my head under the covers. We heard his sleigh bells and knew he was in the area. Each year we heard the bells until Thompson's dog died and the chain holding him to his kennel ceased to rattle.

Of course, we never went to sleep — but we always woke up.

"Walt, Walt, he's been!" Herbert whispered excitedly.

Four o'clock in the morning; feeling down, down into the icy cold pillow slips hanging full of wrapped excitement. The smell of oranges, apples, marry-me-quick. The rustle of paper, sharp corners of wrapped boxes, cold feet on icy lino. We tore at the paper to discover the magic within; selection boxes full of *spice*, were opened well before daybreak and the chocolatey contents partly devoured in the cold dark. Excitedly we showed mum and dad what he'd brought us, *he* now being relegated to someone we needn't be good for until a few weeks before the following Christmas.

Christmas dinner — what a feast. We had roast rabbit, potatoes, cabbage, stuffing, Yorkshire Pudding and gravy. Mum brought in the Christmas pudding and tipped it out of its white chipped basin onto the centre plate. It was scrumptious. I'd watched mum make it weeks before using the rationed currants and raisins, suet, carrot and lots of other ingredients. When it was mixed and ready, it was slowly cooked in the copper in the corner of the kitchen. We watched the fire carefully to make sure it didn't go out. All day it bubbled away, filling the house with its heady, rich smell.

After dinner we played with our toys. One year dad made us a tank each. We sat in them, and out in the yard, fought World War Two. I resented being the *Germans*. Herbert was always the *British*. I'd drive my tank hard at his, shouting all the time, "Achtung! Achtung!" ramming him as he let fly with his turret gun. I was desperate to win but knew in my heart *Germans* never won, not in our gang. I was doomed, even before the battle. I played the Germans only on the promise that he'd be them next time. Next time never materialised.

*

"Lord, the tide's come in and everybody's happy."

"He didn't say that, you burk. He said, 'Lo, I bring you tidings of great joy to all mankind'."

"Well, I knew it was something like that," Enoch sulked.

"I don't know," Alan went on, "We'll never have this play right if you can't remember what yer supposed to say."

He turned to Herbert who was lolling by Uncle George's garden hut, sucking the end of his spear.

"You're supposed to be an angel as well," he remonstrated. "We agreed that yesterday. You and Enoch are angels. Rosie is Mary. Brian and Barry are the Three Wise Men, and Margaret is all the sheep and other animals. We agreed that. Now look, you've come dressed as a Roman Soldier. There weren't any soldiers about when he was born."

"I like being a soldier though," Herbert replied, "You know I like killing."

"Well you can't. You're an angel and that's that... or you'll not play."

Herbert was sulking now. "Can't I just kill a sheep then?" he asked. "They killed sheep as human sacrifices. Miss Fillibut told us in Religious Education last week."

"Yer not touching me with that spear," Margaret exclaimed.

"No, you can't kill a sheep," Alan answered. "Now come on or we'll never be ready for the show."

It had been Rosie's idea to put on a show for our parents as a surprise for Christmas. At first we'd jeered at the idea, but Rosie's cajoling and persistence had won the day and so now here we all stood in varying degrees of biblical dress in Uncle George's back yard ready for a rehearsal.

Rosie sat on an upturned bucket quietly picking at a scab on her knee. Beside her was an onion crate stuffed with straw from the rabbit hutch. In the centre lay her black doll.

"Right," Alan said. "Let's start. Margaret you're supposed to be by the manger."

Margaret hitched up her mother's old shopping frock, crossed the yard and knelt at the side of the onion crate.

"That's right," Alan smiled, "Now start making yer animal noises."

Margaret knelt on all fours and began barking and meowing.

"Not dogs and cats, burk," Alan shouted. "Sheep and donkeys! Dogs and cats weren't there when he was borned, you know that, I showed you that picture yesterday. There were no dogs and cats on it were there? Now do a donkey."

Enoch giggled.

"I can't make a donkey noise," Margaret answered. "I can only do dogs and cats."

Alan sighed and said, "Oh, all right then I suppose they'll have to do."

Meanwhile Brian and Barry had moved to the lank grass and squatted opposite each other, pretending to warm their hands on an invisible fire.

"It's cold in t'desert tonight, in't it?" Barry said to Brian.

"Yeah," Brian answered, "Mind you, don't forget it's winter. Lucky we an't had any snow."

Barry nodded. "Nowt much happens around here, does it? Just sheep to look after and sand to play in – roll on Christmas."

Suddenly Enoch's and Herbert's voices boomed from Uncle George's lavatory roof. Both Three Wise Men looked up. Enoch stood with his arms above his head in the stance of an angel from heaven.

"Lord, I bring you turnings of great kind about a baby who's been born in Beflelum. Just nar.".

"What do you want us to do about it?" Barry asked, feigning fear.

"What you've got to do is pack yer sheep up and go and see him. Oh, before I go, don't forget to tek him some presents. You know it's Christmas."

"Righto," Brian said. "What would he like?"

"Oh you can get him some gold and Frankie's scent and, er... what were that other one?" Enoch asked Herbert.

Herbert thought for a moment then said, "Was it a spear?"

Enoch shook his head. "I can't think of the other one. You'll have to buy him something on the way there."

"It's night time don't forget," Barry said. "Shops will be shut. And also they don't open at Christmas."

Brian nodded in agreement.

Enoch thought for a while, brightened and said, "Lo. You can buy him something after Christmas. Tell him that. Say that the angels said it would be okay. We're off back to heaven now."

"See you," Brian called.

Enoch and Herbert jumped from the roof and landed behind the garden hut.

"I suppose we'd better get going. It's a long way to Beflelum," Barry said.

They stood and began walking up and down until they judged that they had covered the requisite distance, then, turning, they walked towards Rosie.

"'Ullo," Brian said. "Are you Mary?"

Rosie raised her head from tending the baby and answered, in a sweet angelic voice, "Yes, that is me."

"Oh," Brian continued, "well, we've come to look at yer baby. Angels sent us. They said to bring him these presents."

"Who are you?" Rosie breathed.

"We're the Three Wise Men but there's only two of us, so Barry's playing the part of the other one."

"Enter my stable. All are welcome," Rosie said with a religious air. "Joseph fetch them a chair."

She turned back to the Three Wise Men, "Joseph is my husband, he's a joiner, he makes things from wood."

Alan stopped tapping on a piece of wood, put his dad's cobbling hammer on the ground and fetched two house bricks for the weary travellers.

"Rest a while," Rosie spoke, "Take the weight off yer feet. You two Three Wise Men are allus welcome."

Brian and Barry sat on the house bricks and peered into

the onion crate. Barry, who was somewhat smaller than Brian, reached forward, and holding the edge of the crib, stretched to look in on the child. The crib was rather unsteady and as he applied his weight it toppled over and crashed to the ground. Rosie jumped up, spilling the brown carrier bag containing the presents to the floor.

"You burk, look what you've done! You've smashed his cot and woke him up. They'll be mad in heaven about this."

Barry mumbled an apology.

Brian leapt to Barry's defence. "Yer husband's a joiner in't he? He can mend the cot, he's only got to fetch his tools."

"Men don't work at Christmas, you know that, it's a holiday," Rosie shot back. "He'll have nowhere to sleep until the New Year because of you."

"Soz," Barry apologised again.

"It dun't matter," Alan broke in, "Pretend the cot is fixed. Let's carry on." Rosie sulked for a moment, mumbled, "Alright," then sat once more on her house brick.

"What you brought him then?" she snapped.

"We've brought him some of Frankie's scent, some gold, and a present that we'll get him after Christmas 'cos shops are shut," Brian answered brightly.

Margaret, who up to this point had remained quiet, suddenly barked loudly.

"The sheep are a bit restless tonight," Joseph said, "it must be all the excitement of having visitors."

Margaret barked again, then meowed as Alan stroked her hair.

"There, there," Alan soothed, "It's only Three Wise Men with some presents for the baby."

Suddenly Enoch and Herbert appeared on the lavatory roof again. Both held their arms above their heads.

"Lo!" Enoch shouted, "we've come back."

"Fear not everybody," Herbert called, "We've come to tell you summat else, an't we?"

He turned to angel Enoch. Enoch nodded.

"What you got to tell us, oh angels from heaven?" Rosie bellowed.

"It's this," Herbert answered, "There's a King called Harold, and he's looking for all the babies in the desert."

"What for?" Rosie asked.

"Don't know," Herbert answered

"You must know," Rosie accused, "Yer from heaven aren't you? They know everything that's going on down here do heaven's people."

"Well, we don't," Enoch shouted, "All we were supposed to do was to tell you."

Herbert nodded vigorously to support Enoch's statement.

"If he kills all the babies," Rosie said, "There'll be nobody left to grow up."

The Three Wise Men pondered this great truth for some moments then Barry offered, "We'll smuggle you and yer baby away to a secret place where King Harold can't find you. He can grow up there."

Joseph stopped hitting his wood with the hammer and began packing imaginary belongings into the carrier bag. "We'd better mek sharp," he said. "Climb on the donkey and we'll be off."

Rosie stood and straddled Margaret. "I'm ready," she called.

"You've forgotten the baby," Brian pointed out. Joseph reached and handed the doll to Rosie.

Lowering herself onto Margaret's back, she clicked her teeth and commanded, "Giddy up!"

Margaret's knees pressed into the tarmac, the pain was too much and she collapsed to the ground, spilling Mary and the baby to one side. The Three Wise Men laughed. Rosie lay fuming.

"It's not funny you know," she snapped. "I've hurt me elbow." She twisted her arm and examined the raw graze that began to ooze blood. The sight of the wound and the delayed stinging pain, triggered tears in her eyes, and she sobbed. "I'm going home," she whimpered.

Regaining her feet, Mary walked down the entry dragging the doll behind her. The gang watched her leave in silence, realising the nativity play was now effectively cancelled. Slowly the angels crossed the yard. Margaret stood, and Alan threw the wood together with his trade, into the long grass. The Three Wise Men reseated themselves on the house bricks and shared a piece of three day old chewing gum.

"Well," Alan said, "that's that!"

"I'm not bothered," Margaret spoke. "I didn't fancy carrying Rosie around on me back anyway, she weighs a ton."

We all nodded. "We'd better give the rabbit its straw back, I bet it's cold," Brian said.

"It won't matter if it's cold or not soon. Dad's going to kill it to celebrate Christmas with," Barry answered.

"Just like King Harold did to all them babies," Margaret said quietly.

"Can I come and watch?" Herbert the angel asked eagerly.

"Watch what?"

"Yer dad killing the rabbit."

"If you want."

"Thanks Barry. Thanks ever so much. Wow, I can't wait for Christmas to come!"

They approached the hutch, each carrying a handful of straw. First the angels, then the Three Wise Men, then Joseph, and lastly, the animals of the nativity. Far away the faint sound of the Salvation Army Band could be heard playing, *Away In A Manger*.

Herbert bent close to the wire netting of the rabbit hutch and said quietly, "King Harold's coming to wring yer neck for Christmas."

*

After the war Dad exhumed the air raid shelter and erected it next to the lavatory to serve as a junk shed. That's where 'The Palmer Film Studios' were born and died. My film camera was an upturned bicycle supported on two house bricks. I turned the pedals slowly so that the back wheel could take up the 'film'. The lens was a cardboard tube which I peered through at Rosie Bacon and my cousin Barry as they self-consciously acted, dressed in cast-off grown up clothes.

The trouble with Rosie was that she was preoccupied with other people's 'naughty bits' and would be forever changing the script to include a crafty look at the aforementioned. Each time this happened I would shout "Cut!" Very professional that, I picked it up from an American film that mum took us to see. Rosie would sulk and threaten to go home and we'd have to promise her a look when we'd finished filming, before she'd go on.

We filmed shipwrecks, wars, cowboys, *Robin Hood*, in fact we were more productive than Metro Goldwyn Mayer, but you could always be sure, Rosie would work in a 'Doctors and Nurses' scene somewhere along the way. Any pretext and she was at it.

"I think the bullet's gone through the top of his leg, sir," she'd shout. "I'll have a look and cure it."

Bullets, arrows, cannonballs all seemed to find their way to the "top of his leg, sir," with Rosie. And the times she was having a baby in a film were endless. *Robin Hood* was always to blame and Rosie couldn't wait to become Mrs Hood. How Barry suffered in the cause of film art! Rosie's knickers were navy blue, and none too clean at that. We knew because she was forever showing us them. Her breasts were non-existent but she'd stuff paper down her frock and pretend. Rosie was an ordeal and always brought chaos to the film set if the film didn't end with a wedding scene.

In winter the studio and film crew were allowed to use the front room, by special dispensation from mum. The camera was set up in one corner of the empty room and an old blackout curtain was hung up to the window. Over a period of time, using old biscuit and Ostermilk tins we made studio lights and plugging them in to the ceiling rose, dangerously overloaded the ancient wiring system.

We filmed pirate stories using buckets of water to splash Rosie, calling it sea spray. That film was never finished. Rosie's mother came up to our house and played hell with mum because Rosie had gone home drenched and crying. We hid in the lavatory, giggling, till the coast was clear, but it still cost me a clipped ear.

Barry suggested a *Tarzan* film. We screwed a cuphook into the ceiling and tied a piece of washing line to it. I filmed him through the cardboard tube as he swung through the air and watched as half the ceiling crashed in on *Tarzan*. Mum rushed in.

"What you two been doing?"

"It just fell in mam, honest."

We became friendly with the projectionist at the Darnall 'Bug Hut',and after the penny rush on Saturdays we waited outside the side door for him. He was a smashing man and allowed us to look at the huge projectors in the projection room. We were fascinated and he was proud that someone was interested in his job. He gave us lengths of old film which we treasured and used on our film set. They were mostly 'British Board Of Film Censor' leaders but to us it was proper professional film — to be prized.

The film studios finally closed one bright Sunday afternoon. We were filming on location, another fascinating word I'd learned from the *Picture Goer* magazine. We were on the flat part of the ruined church filming the war. The Thompsons had just suffered a terrible defeat at the hands of 'Achtunging' Tommy Turner. Barry was on his way to rescue them when the gang from the top of Coleford Road invaded us for real. After a brief, brave, show of fighting, stones filling the air, we fled. Our 'camera' was carried off as the spoils of war and Rosie Bacon went home crying, her head split open by a piece of skimmed slate. After that my preoccupation with films and theatre was enjoyed alone.

*

"I'm getting some tickets for the kids' outing with the club," dad told mum.
Our ears pricked up and we stopped eating.
"Get on with your tea, you two."
"Where we going dad. When?" we chorused.
"Eat your tea, I said. How many times do I have to tell you, no talking at the table!" mam scolded.
Dad spoke; "I think they're going to Cleethorpes, next week."
"Wow! Cleethorpes! Where's Cleethorpes dad?"
"It's seaside."
"Wow! Seaside!"
"Eat your tea, I said, and take your elbows off the table, else you'll not be going anywhere!" mam retorted.
We bent our heads to the plates and wolfed the remaining food down.
"Finished!" we cried.
"And?" mam asked.
"Oh yes, pleasemayIleavethetable?"
"Yes."
Slipping from the chairs, we crowded around dad.
"What's seaside dad?" we asked.
"Well." said dad, "there's a lot of water like, and it comes in and goes out, all day it does that, in, out, in, out. Although," he said under his breath, "I've heard it said that tide doesn't come in at Cleethorpes; it gives itself up from exhaustion. Anyway, that's where you're going for the day with the club."
The Club, as dad called it, was the Darnall Aqueduct Working Men's Club, commonly shortened to 'The Ackerdock'. Once a year the club organised a kids' outing to the coast, paid for out of the subscriptions and profits of its

members. All the local Clubs competed to outdo each other with their generousity towards members' kids. The outings were grand affairs.

On the day of departure our parents took us down to the club. Outside, the charabancs were lined up along the roads and side streets.

Large labels were tied to buttonholes, giving the coach number, the name and address of the wearer and the name of the club. Stewards for the day shepherded us to our coach and handed us aboard, while parents gave last minute advice to offspring.

"Don't you go paddling when the tide's going out."
"Don't go on too many fairground rides."
"Don't eat too much and be sick on the coach."
"Don't lose your money."
"Don't lose your brother/sister."
"Listen what coach you've gone on."
"Remember what coach station you get off at."
"Don't lose your label."
"Don't talk to strangers."
"Go to the lavatory in twos."

And finally, as an afterthought, they'd add; "Oh, and have a good time; and don't worry, we'll be here when you come back."

Of course, the minute the coaches turned the end of the road all advice was forgotten and the lunch packs handed to each passenger were devoured within one minute flat.

As the journey progressed the coach steward stood up at ten minute intervals and asked, "Does anybody want to go to the lavatory?"

This was answered with a chorus of; "Not me mester, I don't," effectively drowning out the weak voices of; "Yes please, I do."

In consequence, seats became damp and the air foetid.

"Are you sure nobody wants to go to the lavatory?" We were now forty-five miles into the journey and the steward was beginning to marvel at our bladder control. He leaned to the driver and spoke, "Better stop Alf or you'll have a flooded coach." The driver stopped at the next convenient field and out we trooped. Ablutions over, back to the bus, boys with nettled legs, girls with nettled bottoms.

"He's sitting in my seat."
"No I'm not, I've sat here all the way."
"No you haven't, that's me sister's seat! Gerrup!"

"Shan't!"

"I'll get you when we get off the chara!"

"Thee and whose army?"

Fists flew, chaos at the back of the coach.

"Pack it in you lot or I'll turn the chara round and you'll not go!" the steward shouted. "Alright Alf, take it away."

A trembling voice spoke from half way down the aisle, "I can't find me sister mester, don't leave her."

"Hold it, Alf, somebody's missing."

He marched down the aisle to where a small boy stood. "What's your sister's name, son?"

"Mary, mester."

"Did she get off with the rest of you?"

"I think so."

"Alf, we'll have to look for her."

"What's your second name son?"

"Taylor."

"Right," he shouted, "When I call your names answer them!" He proceeded to call the roll and when he'd accounted for everybody, except Mary Taylor, things were beginning to look rather serious.

"Right," he said, "everybody stop on the chara while I go and look outside."

He left and we all watched through the window as he searched the field looking for Mary.

A small girl walked to Alf and whispered in his ear. Alf turned and said, "Well why didn't you say so earlier!" He blasted his horn and the steward came running.

He clambered aboard breathless; "What's up?"

Alf said, "I think you'd better take a look on the back seat." The steward approached the rear of the coach and saw in a corner a sleeping, curled up, little girl. He bent over her and shook her shoulder. She opened her eyes.

"Are you Mary Taylor?"

"Yes," she said.

And so with the crashing of gears and a roar from the engine we were on our way again.

"We're nearly there now kids, so settle down," the steward shouted.

This was entirely the wrong thing to say to a load of already over-excited youngsters. Everyone scrambled to the windows to shouts of: "I can see the sea."

"That's not sea, you burk, it's only a pond."

"Where's sea then?"

"We haven't come to it yet!" said one knowledgeable boy, "I came last year, sea's at the end of this road, round the corner, if it's in."

What did he mean? Did someone actually bring it to Cleethorpes when visitors were due? If no-one had told them we were coming perhaps the sea would be missing and we'd have nowhere to paddle. Eventually we rounded a corner and there in front of us was The Sea. We marvelled — all that water, it stretched for miles; flat and grey.

"There's some donkeys on the sands, look!"

We followed a pointed, grubby finger and saw four tired looking, moth eaten donkeys trudging on the brown strip of sand followed by a boy who lashed at their backsides with a stick. The coach turned through a pair of large wooden gates and the sea was lost from view. The charabanc shuddered to a stop.'

'Sit in your seats everybody!" the steward ordered. "Right now, as you get off you'll be handed a card of tear-off tickets. These you can use on the fairground rides. Also, each of you will be handed a pound note."

There were "wows" and "oohs" from us. A whole pound note to spend!

"Also," he continued, "you'll get your tea ticket for your tea at the cafe. Don't lose it and be there at five o'clock. Now the cafe's at the top of Station Road. Don't be late!"

As we disembarked he handed us an envelope each, which we tore open to examine the contents.

"Where you going first, Palmer?"

"Don't know."

"We're going to the fair to spend our tickets! Is tha coming?"

Herbert and I tagged along with a group of about six. The leader, who'd been before, showed us the way. We walked along the sea front towards the fairground in the distance. Music was blasting from the arcades, heady smells of fish and chips filled the air, and men leaned over stalls enticing us to "Try your luck son."

"Don't go on them, save your tickets for the rides."

The rides were enormous contraptions all gaudy paint and blaring music and youths who stood on them nonchalantly, at a crazy angle as the machines spun and bucked around.

"Wow! Don't they go fast!"

"I'm not going on that one, it's too fast!"

"Coward!"

"I'm not, I just don't fancy it that's all."

"Coward!"

We stood watching kids from early coaches slowly turning green as the rides gathered speed. This was fun? No wonder the tickets were free!

"I'm going on the *Popeye*, are you?"

"Alright."

We didn't know what the *Popeye* was but it sounded alright. Reaching it we saw a moon rocket with empty seats. At the top sat *Popeye* on a smaller moon rocket.

We clambered in and, sitting in twos, we were off. Slowly we ascended, to be met by a grotesquely grinning Popeye on his way down. At the top, the ride gathered speed until we were spinning round faster and faster. *Popeye* passed us twice at each revolution and his face became more hateful as fear and sickness gripped us.

Round and round, round and round.

The lemonade and the sandwiches were fighting each other inside our vertigoed tummys. One by one we turned first green then white. Just as we were about to lose control the ride started to slow down. Our senses returned as it came to a standstill. We clambered shakily off and stood looking back at grinning *Popeye*.

"Great weren't it?"

"Smashing!"

"Shall we go on it again?"

"No, not yet, let's try something else." *Popeye* wasn't having any more of my tickets.

The day sped past in exploring all the delights of Cleethorpes. On our way to the sands we passed Rosie Bacon who was staring in a gift shop window with rapt attention.

"What you buying us, Rosie?"

"Sod off!"

"What you looking at Rosie?"

"Sod off!"

"Look what Rosie's looking at!" We all gathered around her.

"I weren't looking at that, I were looking for a present for me mam."

'That' was a gold painted plaster statue of a nude boy sporting a corkscrew for its naughty bit!

"You dirty dog, Rosie! Fancy looking at that!"

"I weren't, I tell you! I were looking for a present!"

"Come off it Rosie, we all know you!"

"Yer rotten! Yer all rotten! Leave me alone!" Rosie stormed off up the sea front.

"Hey," said Harry Churchyard, "We haven't bought any presents yet."

Guilt entered our heads.

"Let's go in and buy some ."

"How much is this, mester?"

"What's this cost, mester?"

"Can I have this for two shillings?"

"Look at this! This is alright, I'll have this."

It was a comb in a case and on the front was stamped 'To the Best Mum In the World'. On the reverse was written 'A Present From Cleethorpes'. It was the first time I had bought anything for mum and I felt very grown up and important.

"Bet she'll be pleased," I thought as the assistant placed it in a bag with Cleethorpes stamped on it. I watched my half crown disappear into a drawer.

"It's for me mam, miss," I said grandly.

"Suppose it is, after all it does say so on the case." she answered with her nose in the air. I looked abashed and hurried from the shop feeling hot and embarrassed.

"Where to now?" Herbert asked.

"Let's go and paddle in the sea."

We ran across the road, climbed the green painted railings and dropped onto the sands. We removed our shoes and socks. The odour of hot feet hung around us and the sand flies were in ecstasy.

"Race you to the sea!"

We were up and running across the warm dry beach towards the sound of waves breaking and girls screaming. As we reached the edge of the tide line I was surprised how cold it had become. The North Sea was ice cold and I marvelled at men brave enough to swim out into the brown waves.

"Captain Webb swum the channel from here, tha knows" Alan Thompson said.

"Bet he were cold."

"No, he covered hisself with lard and he had somebody in a boat that made him hot tea and sandwiches all the way. It were dead easy."

"How did he get back?"

"Swum it of course! He were a great swimmer, were

Captain Webb! That's why they've put his face on matchboxes. It reminds everybody when they have a fag what a good swimmer he were, for our Country."

"Bet he's rich, selling all them matches for hisself."

"Course he is, that's how he gets paid for swimming Channel for our Country. Every time you buy a box of matches they send Captain Webb your penny for him and his missus, Mrs Webb. That's what he lives on, boxes of matches. They're dead rich."

"Where's he live?"

"Seaside, of course! He has to be handy to practise every day in the water. I expect he's out there now, practising, covered in lard and drinking tea.

What a great job Captain Webb had got, we decided, then got on with our paddle.

"It's cold, in't it?"

"It's great when you get used to it, look at me!" shouted Alan.

He stood up to his knees in the liquid ice. He was slowly turning blue. My feet eventually became covered, and I thought that that was very daring.

"Come on, son, go in deeper, it's grand."

A large, beer-bellied man ran past and charged into the sea, drenching Alan Thompson. It was the steward of our coach. We watched him belly flop into a wave then surface gasping and thrashing. He'd turned blue and his heart must have been made of iron to withstand the shock of his once a year immersion in the arctic waters. He stood and stumbled his way back to the water's edge. He was shivering and sported a grazed, raw belly.

"By, that were grand," he trembled, then raced back up the beach. I watched him and when he thought he was at a safe distance he stopped, bent double, and held his injured stomach. "Well, he wasn't Captain Webb," I decided.

"Hey, what time is it?" Harry asked.

"Don't know."

"What about our tea at the cafe? Steward said we had to be there at five o'clcock."

We were sitting on the sea front railings, eating toffee apples and thawing out our feet. The sand flies had long since deserted us for richer pickings among the whelk stalls now that we had imprisoned our feet once more in our boots.

"We'd better ask somebody."

A couple strolled past arm in arm.

"Do you know what time it is, mester?"

"Yes, thank you," he answered, and walked on giggling to his girl friend as she appreciated this giant among wits.

"Clever sod!" shouted Alan. The man turned round and we ran.

Eventually we reached Station Road and at the top saw a queue stretching away from a large cafe.

"We're in time anyway," said Herbert as we joined the end of the line.

"Have your tickets ready! No ticket, no tea!" a steward shouted.

The doors opened and we surged forward to the smell of fish and chips. Inside were long tables on which sat dozens of vinegar and salt pots. Blue and white squared oil cloth was drawing-pinned to the wood and smears of brown sauce, dried and crusty, completed the place settings. All six of us dived for a table and scraping the chairs back, we sat down. The cafe filled quickly and soon it was bedlam. A chant started and gathered strength.

"We want our chips! We want our chips."

Stewards tried in vain to restore some semblance of order. From a side door trooped about thirty women all dressed in black and wearing small white aprons. A picture of mum shot into my head. They each carried four plates piled high with chips and enormous battered fish. Everyone was quickly served and the sound of steel on pottery filled the air.

"Look at the size of my fish! I bet it's a whole one."

"Don't you want your peas? I'll have them if you don't."

Food changed plates until some had all chips, some had all fish, and one peculiar spotty lad had all peas. Everything was wolfed down and Grimsby Fish Docks were back on overtime to replenish their depleted stocks. Captains of trawlers could sleep easy in their beds knowing that their catches were being devoured and the crew could sleep and dream of nets full of fish and chips and mushy peas.

After the meal we all sat there full and feeling rather greasy. The head steward got to his feet, and banging a vinegar bottle hard on the table, called for quiet.

"Now, lads and lasses I'm sure you've all had a good tea and are feeling full. What I'd like to say is to thank all the staff and managers here at the Cuddly Cod Cafe for providing such a welcome repast and to thank the waitresses who have served us all. When you get back I hope you all tell your dads and mothers what a good day you've had here at Cleethorpes. Now as a special treat we've got a surprise for you. The club has provided a turn for you to see. He's a conjuror from China, and he's going to do his tricks for you so I want you all to be quiet for him. Here he is, Mr Ali Wong!"

In strode a man dressed in a flowing robe with dragons embroidered down the back and a patch on one of the elbows. He stood bowing repeatedly with his hands up his sleeves. He straightened and pulled a bunch of flowers out of one sleeve. A flower caught on a piece of cotton and snagged the cloth.

"Ah so! Ah so!" he breathed.

"Arse hole! Arse hole!" whispered Tommy Turner and we collapsed laughing.

"Ladelys an gennaman, my next trick was passed to me by an ancient Chinese uncle, is called the magic clylinder. Ah so! Ah so!" He took a metal tube from the table which stood behind him and showed it empty. "Ah so! Ankerchives, velly plity!"

He pulled dozens from the tube and these were followed by flags of the world all joined together. So far not a clap. A bead of sweat showed above his plaited moustache.

"Ah so, Ah so! Now ladelys an gennaman, I would like to show you the Mysterious Cabinet what I've brought all the way from the mysterious East."

"I wonder if his uncle's inside it?" Tommy muttered.

He giggled.

The steward stood up. "Keep it quiet at the back please, or I'll clip your ear'oles!"

Mr Ali Wong bowed to the steward and said; "Thank you velly much, Sid," then turning back to his audience shouted "The Mysterious Cabinet!"

A woman, thinly disguised as a Chinese person, pushed on a large red and black wobbly cabinet. One of its wheels squeaked. Someone at the far end of the room shouted; "Hey mester! It's full of mouses!" Gales of laughter. Mr Ali Wong raised his arms above his head and in a grand gesture shouted again.

"The Mysterious Cabinet." His moustache slipped a fraction of an inch and we became obsessed with it. "Ladeleys and gennamen, I would now like a volunteer from the audience to assist me, Ah so! Ah so!"

He looked around and spotted Rosie, who was stretching herself in her seat in the hopes of stardom.

"Ah, young ladeley, you will do." he said.

Rosie shot forward towards Mr Ali Wong. She stood preening herself by his side.

"Don't disappear forever, Rosie! " Harry shouted.

Rosie ignored the comment.

"I will now place this young English girl in the cabinet and say the magic words."

Mrs Wong moved forward and roughly, but with a false smile, half guided and half pushed Rosie into the black cabinet. Mr Wong whispered something quickly in Rosie's ear and she nodded. He swished shut the curtain across the front of the wobbly box.

"Ladeleys and gennamen, The Mysterious Cabinet."

He made exaggerated passes across the front of the curtain with his hands whilst Mrs Wong pranced from side to side.

"Simsalabim! Ah so!"

He threw back the curtain and Rosie was gone. We sat up and took notice.

"That were good!"

He then removed all the panels until only the framework remained. No Rosie. We clapped and cheered and stamped our feet. Ali Wong was brilliant we decided. He stood basking in the thunderous applause. Mrs Wong pranced and pointed first at her husband and then at the cabinet. We cheered on.

"Ladeleys an gennamen," he roared 'Tank you, tank you!" The applause subsided. "I will now return the young English girl back to the land of the living."

Quickly he and his wife rebuilt the cabinet and when complete he made the now familiar pass across its front, "Simsalabim" and threw back the curtain.

No Rosie. He repeated the farce. Still no Rosie.

"Ladeleys and gennamen, it would appear that the little girl is gone forever!" We ooohed and aahed.

"But, no! Wait!" He held his forehead. "I'm getting a message through from the other side. Ah so! Yes! Yes! No! Yes! Aah! Ladeleys and gennamen, my ancient uncle has sent me a message. He says the little girl is alright and to say the magic word again but this time all together. Are you ready? One, two, three, Simsalabim!"

There was a bright flash and a cloud of white smoke

curled into the air. Mr Ali Wong pointed, "There she is."

All heads turned to the back of the cafe and we saw Rosie dressed in a Chinese cloak. She was standing on a table. We clapped and clapped. Mr and Mrs Wong bowed and left, pushing the Mysterious Wobbly Cabinet in front of them.

"Right children it's time to get back on the coaches. I want you to leave the cafe and form up in the road outside into your coach numbers what's written on your coat tags," the steward announced. "No larking about or you'll get left!"

The cafe emptied quickly and outside groups soon formed. Names were shouted from prepared lists and when each party was complete they marched into the coach park and boarded their respective charabancs.

"That's my seat, I had it coming."

"You haven't booked it, it's anybody's"

"I said it's mine, now get up!"

"Shan't."

"Tha will!"

"I won't!"

Once again, hostilities broke out at the rear of the chara, till the victor took possession of the contested seat.

"Are we all here?" the steward who was not Captain Webb shouted.

Gears crashed and the coach lurched away from Cleethorpes and towards Sheffield. The journey home was uneventful except for three lots of vomiting, seven wet seats, two fights, four broken ash trays, and a nervous breakdown suffered by He Who Was Not Captain Webb.

Our coach rounded the corner at the bottom of the club road and we saw hundreds of parents — well, actually mostly mothers, fathers already being in the club and well tanked up. We all disembarked and mothers claimed offspring. "Did you have a good time?"

"Did you behave?"

"Did you get in any trouble?"

"Did you get your tea?"

"Did you paddle?"

"I've brought you a present mam."

"Oooh love, you shouldn't have! Look at this, it's lovely! I'll always treasure it. Come on, we'll join your dad in the club, he's saved us a seat."

The night wore on until it was chucking out time. My eyes were as heavy as lead and I kept dozing off.

"You'll have to carry him home, he's nearly asleep."

The feeling of being hoisted into the air to straddle dad's shoulders. The smell of Brilliantine on his head as my cheek rested there, pins and needles as legs numbed and the walk home began.

Cold night air... shivering.

House lights, stairs, sheets being tucked in. Whispered "Good night, God Bless." Warm bed. Sand between toes. Sleep.

Mum and dad had decided to move from Darnall to the Manor Estate and a more modern house. When the big day arrived, 139 Coleford Road looked strangely bare. Only the lino that was nailed to the floorboards remained and of course, the coal in the coal cellar. Carpets were rolled and stacked in the yard. The upstairs windows had been removed to allow mum's wardrobe to be lowered to the pavement, and the beds followed suit. Tea chests stood in odd corners, full of pots and pans, glass ornaments, plates, and all the other paraphernalia that had been bought and treasured over the years.

The large removal van arrived and our possessions were quickly loaded aboard, disappearing into its cavernous depths. What had looked a lot now occupied only a quarter of the interior.

All was ready and we climbed excitedly into the driver's cab to sit between the driver and his mate. People were out to see us off and the gang stood shouting and waving to us. The engine started with a roar and a shudder and slowly we slid away from the kerb to start the journey to 145 Beaumont Road, Manor Estate.

I was dumped among the tea chests, chin high in twitch grass in a large overgrown garden. I watched as our possessions were taken into the new house and felt depressed and alone.

People were watching our arrival from behind net curtains and neighbourhood dogs sniffed around us. Dad had a day off work for the flitting and laboured all day pushing furniture around to mum's orders. By dinnertime, with much cursing and swearing and banging with the bed spanner, the two beds were up and erected in their respective bedrooms. Mine and Herbert's was at the rear of the house overlooking a tiny back garden. The room was much bigger than our former one and light flooded in through a large window. Mum and dad took the front bedroom overlooking Beaumont Road.

Teatime arrived to the sound of the wireless, now working. Carpets down and curtains up. The kitchen had a brown stone sink under the window and real hot water on tap. In the corner of the kitchen and opposite the back door, was the coal hole, a fact that was to annoy mum each time the coal man trailed through with his delivery over her clean floor. Off the kitchen was the ultimate luxury, a real bathroom. The toilet was semi-inside, being a porch outside the kitchen door. The pantry was in the living room under the stairs. The house must have been planned when the architect was drunk.

Our first night under the new roof was strangely quiet and restless. We had been brought up with the steady thump, thump of the steel works drop forge hammer going day and night, except on Christmas Day, and the factory hooters and sirens calling the men to work. But now nothing, except the occasional bark from a dustbin-foraging dog. Real silence. Every creak and groan from the house was amplified as it settled for the night. We snuggled down and fell asleep wondering if there was a gang available and, if so, would we be allowed to join?

MARGARET, ME, ALAN, BARRY, ROSE, HERBERT, BRIAN.